Essays that got the world talking

2023 A YEAR OF CONSEQUENCE

EDITED BY JUSTIN BERGMAN

Thames & Hudson | THE CONVERSATION

We wish to acknowledge the Traditional Owners of the land where the authors and editors of this book live and work. Particularly, we wish to acknowledge the traditional owners of the land on which Australia's universities stand, the land on which field work has been conducted, and the land on which much of the research cited in this book has taken place. We pay respects to all Aboriginal and Torres Strait Islander peoples and recognise they are the First Peoples of Australia.

First published in Australia in 2023
by Thames & Hudson Australia Pty Ltd
11 Central Boulevard, Portside Business Park
Port Melbourne, Victoria 3207
ABN: 72 004 751 964

thamesandhudson.com.au

These essays originally appeared on The Conversation (theconversation.com/au).

26 25 24 23 5 4 3 2 1

Thames & Hudson Australia wishes to acknowledge that Aboriginal and Torres Strait Islander people are the first storytellers of this nation and the Traditional Custodians of the land on which we live and work. We acknowledge their continuing culture and pay respect to Elders past and present.

978-1-760-76417-3 (paperback)
978-1-760-76432-6 (ebook)

A catalogue record for this book is available from the National Library of Australia

Cover design: Philip Campbell
Typesetting: Cannon Typesetting
Editing: Paul Smitz
Printed and bound in Australia by McPherson's Printing Group

FSC® is dedicated to the promotion of responsible forest management worldwide. This book is made of material from FSC®-certified forests and other controlled sources.

Contents

PART II On politics and war

PART III Coping with economic pressure

PART VIII Searching for identity and belonging

PART IX Love and loss

Editor's note

Justin Bergman
International Affairs Editor, The Conversation

The book currently in your hands is a selection of the best articles published by The Conversation in 2023. It aims to be three things in one: a collection of compelling writing; a snapshot of Australia and New Zealand's intellectual scene; and a first attempt to make sense of events whose ultimate meaning can only become clear with the passage of time.

As is always the case with The Conversation, the articles have been written by academic experts who draw from a deep well of knowledge and whose work is deftly edited by professional journalists. As always, we are grateful to the selfless authors who put so much time into sharing their ideas and helping us to be informed. This book is theirs.

The work of preparing this edition was complicated by the timing of the unsuccessful referendum on the Indigenous Voice to Parliament. Given the importance of this vote – as well as the likelihood of misinformation surrounding it – we leaned into our mission to inform the public deliberation throughout the year.

We started our coverage by asking readers to send in their questions on the referendum, and they did – more than 9000 of them. We then commissioned our experts at Australian universities – largely First Nations academics and researchers – to answer those questions. We began with the basics: what is the Voice, where did it come from and what can it achieve?

Australia's rejection of the opportunity offered by the Uluru Statement from the Heart is also recorded and analysed here. Sana Nakata describes the arduous journey to get to the referendum and where, in her opinion, it all went wrong. And Bhiamie Williamson says the result is nothing short of a 'political disaster', but there are now opportunities for a new generation of First Nations leaders to push forward with sympathetic yet radical activism.

Elsewhere, too, 2023 has been a year of heavy consequence. A devastating war broke out between Israel and Hamas, while another traumatic conflict, between Russia and Ukraine, lumbered on. It was a time of economic uncertainty, thanks to the ever-higher creeping of inflation rates and soaring prices for everything from groceries to electricity. Housing affordability reached a crisis point, for both buyers and renters.

Change also came in the form of technological innovation, and our authors tackle the questions it raised. Should the development of advanced artificial intelligence be paused? Is it ethical to pour money into life-extension research or have a baby at a time of climate crisis? How much do we really need weight-loss drugs like Ozempic?

The essays here also touch on the way in which ordinary choices can sometimes be consequential, such as how one Bangladeshi immigrant, trained to be an engineer, struggled to start a new life in Australia and found purpose selling homemade pickles.

Like many, I can relate to this. I arrived in Melbourne six years ago with a partner who already had a job lined up. I woke up every morning with the daunting task of reinventing my life in a strange place (albeit one with far better coffee). This year my partner, children and I became citizens of Australia, taking part in a tearful, uplifting ceremony and departing with a packet of wattle seeds to plant wherever we make our home.

I hope these selections convey something of the optimism I feel while paying due regard to the serious challenges we face. There's no telling what 2024 will bring, but I will be planting my wattle seeds and watching them grow.

October 2023

Is the Albanese government making consequential change or just incremental decisions?

Michelle Grattan
Chief Political Correspondent, The Conversation
Professorial Fellow, University of Canberra

Giving Australia's First Nations people a Voice to Parliament enshrined in the Constitution would have been the Albanese government's most consequential social policy achievement in the first half of its current parliamentary term. The Prime Minister believed he could defy the history of multiple failed referendums to pull it off. But it was always a gamble against the odds and, unsurprisingly, he lost the 14 October vote. The rejection was overwhelming. Instead of a hoped-for triumph, the referendum delivered Anthony Albanese his biggest blow in office, following his party's election in May 2022.

Australians are notoriously conservative about altering the Constitution. Since Federation, only eight of the now forty-five proposals put up have passed. None that lacked basic bipartisan support has succeeded, and only one put forward by a Labor government.

Albanese invested much effort and emotion into the Voice cause, and at the start of 2023 the polling looked promising. But the slide was beginning, and it sped up about April when Liberal leader Peter Dutton declared his opposition (although there were a number of high-profile Liberal 'yes' campaigners). In the last week of the campaign, at Uluru, where the Statement from the Heart had been written in 2017, Albanese shed tears.

The referendum vote showed patterns, with the 'yes' case favoured in progressive inner-urban electorates and teal seats. Younger voters and people with higher incomes and education were more likely to vote 'yes'. Outer suburbia, a key battleground for the next election, went for 'no'. So did the regions.

In his speech on referendum night, Albanese took responsibility. He committed the government to continuing to try to 'close the gap' of disadvantage and to promote reconciliation. But many Indigenous leaders were angry and disillusioned, making those commitments all the more challenging for Labor.

While Australia's voters said 'no' to the Voice, opinion polling indicated they were still firmly behind the Albanese government as it approached the halfway point of the parliamentary term. Whatever the ripples from the referendum loss, it won't necessarily have a major impact on how people feel about the government in the longer term. For most voters, the Voice was a second- or third-order issue. At the next election, due by May 2025, they will be focused on their own economic circumstances, the government's general record and their assessment of the Dutton-led alternative.

The Voice defeat, however, may alter the dynamics within the higher reaches of the government, where Albanese has enjoyed untrammelled authority. He is not a details man and accords his ministers considerable freedom within their portfolios. But in broad terms, his judgement has seemed little challenged internally. Post-referendum, some ministers may be more sceptical of that judgement.

Certainly the rejection of the Voice brings into question whether a second-term Labor government would attempt to change the Constitution to move Australia to a republic. That has been Labor's aspiration; it even has a minister for the republic. But it would be a more difficult (and consequential) change to achieve a republic than the Voice originally appeared to be.

Voters remain patient

This year saw the end of the government's honeymoon period, but it was still enjoying a patient electorate. Labor's general performance was strong enough and the memory of Scott Morrison's prime ministership fresh enough (reinforced by revelations that continued to emerge) to protect against any 'voter regret' at the electoral switch of 2022.

Albanese has made good on his election promises, among them cheaper child care and medicines. A new medium-term emissions-reduction target is set in legislation. A worker- and union-friendly industrial relations agenda is being rolled out. A National Anti-Corruption Commission, headquartered in Canberra, started operating in mid-2023. But the government faces growing challenges as it begins to look towards the battle for a second term. With a string of interest rate rises, and inflation still above the Reserve Bank target, many people are under serious cost-of-living pressure.

Wages have started to move a little faster, but rises are largely eaten up by price increases. The federal budget has bounced back, with an expected hefty deficit turning into a fat surplus for 2022–23; the current financial year may also show a surplus. But the economy is slowing, productivity is stuck, and spending on programs – most notably the National Disability Insurance Scheme (NDIS) – has to be contained. This means there will be 'losers'. As many people find it harder to make ends meet, the government has resisted calls for more cost-of-living relief.

To an extent, the past year and a half has been government by inquiry, ranging from a royal commission into the Robodebt scandal to reviews of the arts, migration and education policies and the NDIS. There is also an investigation into the handling of the COVID-19 pandemic, but that has attracted criticism for its narrow terms of reference, which exclude unilateral decisions made by state and territory governments.

For the remainder of this term, the government's emphasis must be on delivery. A testing challenge will be the transition to a clean-energy economy, which is proceeding more slowly than required to meet the government's target of having renewables provide 82 per cent of national electricity generation by 2030.

There is no chance of Labor fulfilling its pre-election commitment of an average $275 fall in household electricity bills by 2025. The Opposition argues nuclear energy will become both viable and required to reach the target of net-zero emissions by 2050. This will make the Coalition – which has yet to produce an energy policy – a potential target of a scare campaign. The government dismisses the idea of nuclear energy for Australia as a fantasy and won't even lift the ban on it. It says to do so would be a distraction, but the reality is it does not want to stir its anti-nuclear base.

The housing challenge

In many areas, the Albanese government requires, for its objectives, the cooperation of the states, which are now all run by Labor governments with the exception of Tasmania. Housing is a notable example of the federal government providing funds for a policy area, but responsibility for its implementation lies substantially at the state level. Tackling the housing crisis has been impeded by a shortage of labour and supplies, as well as the unwillingness of local councils to approve new developments – just when a high level of net migration (fuelled by the return of overseas students and a voracious demand for workers) means a big boost in stock is needed. On housing, the government is increasingly under pressure from the Greens, who are pitching to be the party for renters.

Albanese won the election by being conservative and appealing to middle Australia. In office, this has so far been a 'Labor' government (with an emphasis on wages, industrial relations and social security) with a notably cautious Prime Minister – apart from the referendum. Albanese believes Labor needs to be a long-term government to bake in significant change. This means avoiding being too forward-leaning in policy – or going back on promises. So welfare benefits were increased in the May 2023 budget (beyond the normal indexation rises), but not by as much as recommended by the government's own Economic Inclusion Advisory Committee. And Albanese has stuck to his election promise to continue with the controversial (and already legislated) Stage 3 tax cuts, which are skewed to higher-income earners, despite calls for them to be scrapped or refashioned.

The gradualist approach has led to criticism from some that Labor should be doing more, taking advantage of the here and now, rather than banking on having more terms during which to implement a reform agenda incrementally. (The New Zealand election in October showed how quickly voter sentiment can change – a Labour landslide in 2020 turned into a conservative wave in 2023.)

Two federal by-elections were held in Australia in 2023, prompted by the retirement of former Liberal ministers. On 1 April, Labor made history in the Melbourne seat of Aston where, for the first time in about a century, a federal government won a seat from the Opposition in a by-election. The result sent shockwaves through the Liberals, underlining their deep unpopularity in Victoria. On the other hand, the Liberals on 15 July easily retained the seat of Fadden in Queensland, the state that remains the conservative heartland.

The Albanese government has lost no ministers to scandals, but its weaker frontbench performers have come under pressure: Linda Burney, Minister for Indigenous Australians, during the referendum campaign, and Catherine King, transport minister, after she rejected Qatar Airways's push for more flights to Australia. The government's best-performing minister, so far, has been Treasurer Jim Chalmers. With leadership ambitions of his own and impressive communications skills, Chalmers is a fiscal conservative who has foreshadowed significant but not radical reforms, including reshaping key economic institutions: the Reserve Bank and the Productivity Commission.

One of the most consequential developments for Australia in 2023 has been the improving relationship with China, which began quickly after the election. This has been driven substantially by how China perceives its wider interests, with the defeat of the Morrison government facilitating a reset. China has progressively lifted trade restrictions on Australian commodities, and Albanese received an invitation to visit Beijing. In October, Australian journalist Cheng Lei, detained in Beijing for three years, was released. Meanwhile, in the Pacific, the government has stepped up Australia's bid for influence with small island states, wary of China's ever-encroaching reach.

As Prime Minister, Albanese has been a constant traveller on the world stage. One of the government's main foreign policy objectives has been maintaining the close relationship with the United States. It is progressing the AUKUS agreement – which will eventually deliver nuclear-powered submarines to Australia – that it inherited from its predecessor. In August, at the first face-to-face ALP national conference in five years, the government fended off some rank-and-file criticism of AUKUS.

Dealing with the crossbench

This parliament has seventeen crossbenchers in the House of Representatives, but they do not have the balance of power, so their clout is strictly limited. Question time remains more or less as predictable and unruly as before, although the expansion of the crossbench does mean a few more probing questions.

The government has been fortunate that, while it does not have a majority in the Senate, the upper house is basically progressive in hue. But the Greens, with their numbers boosted in both houses, have become increasingly assertive. As a result, Labor does not always prevail in the upper house, at least not easily. It had to buy its way out of an impasse over its legislation for a $10 billion Housing Australia Future Fund.

On occasion, the government can be thwarted in the Senate by the non-Greens crossbenchers. The government could not, for example, head off a Senate inquiry into its denial of extra Qatar Airways flights. The government's shifting explanations over its Qatar decision also highlighted that its record on accountability has not lived up to Labor's pre-election promises to be more open and transparent.

The federal Opposition, meanwhile, has been stranded between its (majority) conservative and (minority) small-'l' liberal wings this year. Dutton's eyes are on winning in the outer suburbs, but there's a general belief he can't achieve office without regaining some teal territory (and not losing any more to independent candidates).

Dutton is an unpopular leader, but he's much in the style of Tony Abbott, who showed that unpopularity isn't necessarily a barrier to cutting through with a negative message. Former treasurer Josh Frydenberg's announcement that he would not contest Kooyong at the next election was a blow to those Liberals hoping the party would (at least in the longer term) move more to the centre.

With the caveat that things can change very quickly, there is a general expectation at this point that the Coalition has little prospect of becoming the government at the next election. On the other hand, with Labor having only a small majority, its challenge is to avoid being pushed into minority government, which would further limit its scope for bold decisions.

October 2023

PART I

A consequential decision for the nation

Editor's note: Aboriginal and Torres Strait Islander readers are advised this section refers to deceased Aboriginal people, their words and names. Also, historical language is used that may cause offence.

The political subjugation of First Nations peoples is no longer historical legacy

Sana Nakata
James Cook University

There has never been a decade without a significant Indigenous-led movement in Australia. These movements have centred on the reinstatement of Indigenous peoples' rights as self-determining peoples, and demands for justice arising from our brutal dispossession and its contemporary fingerprints.

There has also never been a successful referendum in Australia without bipartisan support. Success for the Voice to Parliament was always going to be against the odds.

In May 2017, more than 250 community delegates from across the country stood together and provided an invitation to the Australian people through the Uluru Statement from the Heart. The statement proposed a path forward for the nation: Voice, Treaty and Truth.

On 14 October 2023, Australia voted on the first step and, in delivering a 'no', revealed the heart of this nation.

The journey to get here

Megan Davis and George Williams's 2021 book *Everything You Need to Know about the Uluru Statement from the Heart* offers a heartbreaking timeline of the many forms of political claim-making First Nations people have engaged in since at least 1846. These include petitions to kings and queens and to governors, requesting land grants; demands for freedom, autonomy over reserve areas and representation in the parliament; labour strikes; and calls for treaty and land rights.

In the thirteen years since the 2010 Expert Panel on Constitutional Recognition, there have been seven separate processes and ten reports. In the middle of these, the sixth report was the *Final Report of the Referendum Council*, which came shortly after the delivery of the Uluru Statement from the Heart. The report's recommendations focused on constitutional recognition in the form of a Voice to Parliament because this was the most strongly endorsed of the five options considered by the twelve regional deliberative dialogues. The Uluru Statement from the Heart also called for Treaty, the second-most strongly endorsed form of recognition, and for Truth, out of respect for the truth-telling that was given at each and every dialogue.

Where it all went wrong

Years of bipartisan support was maintained until the early months of this year. By February, it was becoming clear that Opposition leader Peter Dutton would be unlikely to support the Voice to Parliament referendum. In doing this, Dutton actively ignored the advice of those around him in the Liberal Party. On 5 April, he announced the Liberals would formally oppose the Voice. Australia would head to its forty-fifth referendum without bipartisan support for the proposal, knowing no referendum had ever succeeded without it.

In August, the *Australian Financial Review*'s Phillip Coorey reported a leaked text message from a coalition MP: 'We can't win the election unless we defeat the Voice solidly. i.e. we need to defeat it to get to the election starting line.' The Opposition made its bet: defeat the Voice and give itself a chance at the next federal election. This transformed a people-driven proposal into a partisan political debate. It made for a campaign characterised by lies, misinformation, disinformation and outright conspiracies circulated on social media platforms. The mainstream media was sometimes complicit in this, either failing to fact-check basic claims or giving misinformation equal weight in their presentation of 'both sides'.

The 'no' campaign's decision to position two prominent Aboriginal faces as its spokespeople enabled a doubly effective claim to division: arguing the Voice would create racial division between Indigenous and non-Indigenous peoples, and that Indigenous people also couldn't agree. The small levels of disagreement within the Aboriginal and Torres Strait Islander community were, so often, treated as media spectacle and not with the seriousness our diverse political views deserve, in the context of so much shared experience.

What now?

We have heard numerous thought bubbles about what happens next, if not a Voice. These have included Dutton's suggestion of a second referendum on symbolic recognition, which he walked away from immediately after the Voice referendum defeat. That proposal would not have had any support from First Nations people. Nor would there have been much appetite for it in the wider Australian population. That lack of support also no doubt informed the Prime Minister's decision not to pursue a legislated Voice.

Senator Lidia Thorpe is likely to call for truth-telling and treaty-making, although those involved in the Victorian processes have thrown their weight behind the necessity of the Voice to give the strongest effect to Treaty and Truth. Whatever comes next, we now know it will happen without a protected representative connection between the community and the Commonwealth Parliament.

There will no doubt continue to be a lot of commentary and analysis in the coming months about the relative successes and failures of the 'no' and 'yes' campaigns, their strategies and their arguments. For most Aboriginal peoples and Torres Strait Islanders, however, this will be of little interest or use. The political subjugation and further marginalisation of First Nations peoples is no longer historical legacy but a contemporary decision reinscribing centuries of paternalism: that we are not peoples deserving of a protected right to be heard on matters that affect us.

We asked for change. We asked to be heard. We asked the Australian people to walk with us. And so now we are where we have always been, left to build our better futures on our own.

The failed referendum is a political disaster, but opportunity exists for those brave enough and willing to embrace it

Bhiamie Williamson
Monash University

The date of 14 October 2023 will be remembered by many as the day reconciliation died. The defeat of the Voice to Parliament referendum may not have surprised many of us Aboriginal and Torres Strait Islander people. After all, we have become accustomed to disappointment. Nonetheless, it was a devastating and demoralising blow.

We must take stock of this political disaster and consider where it leaves us as a nation and a society, and in what direction we walk from here.

A political disaster

I have published extensively on the impacts of disasters such as fires and floods on Indigenous peoples. When a disaster strikes, people's experiences are varied and complicated. Some escape relatively unscathed, perhaps even better off, while others are heavily and negatively affected. It is common for those negatively impacted to experience shock and trauma.

There is much to be learned by viewing the referendum defeat as a political disaster. The first thing to acknowledge is the impact the result will have on many of our peoples and allies. We must validate these feelings of hurt, distress and anger. Yet the opportunities after a disaster lie in the rebuild, in learning and adapting, and in recognising the systemic features of our society that produce vulnerabilities.

Formalising the informal

Many Indigenous people have maintained that Australia is a racist country. This is not to say every person who voted 'no' on 14 October is a racist. Motivations driving individual voting preferences are complicated, contested, perhaps even contradictory. We must be careful not to equate an individual 'no' vote with a marker of individual racism. But ignoring patterns of racism, including the relentless racist dialogue from some in the 'no' campaign, is to be wilfully, and knowingly, indifferent.

Racism is a drug, and Australia has an addiction. Our insistence on this has elicited strong rejections from mainstream Australia, which has preferred to see racist events – the Northern Territory Intervention, the 2005 Cronulla riots, the booing of AFL player Adam Goodes – as isolated instances. For us, these instances are never isolated. They join together in a chain of prejudice that began with the arrival of the First Fleet.

We could say Australia has always been casually, or informally, racist. The resounding 'no' written by the majority of Australians across all states and territories bar one, then, formalises the informal. Finally recognising this fundamental truth about our society will allow us to take generational steps to address it.

Many of us will remember 14 October as a spectacular own goal, rivalling perhaps the Whitlam dismissal. It was a day when, rather than step towards a kinder, more equitable future, Australia chose to retreat to a deeply problematic past.

Where to from here?

Within the disappointment of defeat there remains an opportunity for those brave enough and willing to embrace it. We have been denied a place within the Constitution, but it is within our collective power to reconstitute ourselves and create a self-determined Voice. We don't even need to look far to see how this might work.

Established in 2010, the National Congress of Australia's First Peoples was perhaps the most complete expression of what an organised and unified Voice might be. The congress's decline was not because it wasn't an effective model of representation. Rather, it was disbanded in 2019 because of the withdrawal of funding by a Coalition government. If funding is holding back a self-determined Voice such as a congress, the 'yes' campaign has shown that Indigenous peoples are far from friendless or penniless.

Other opportunities may exist in plain sight. I have previously written about the sleeping electoral power of Indigenous peoples. Could Indigenous votes be mobilised beyond the Northern Territory for targeted political impact?

For those wanting more direct and tangible opportunities, perhaps now is the time to become a donor to charities working with our communities. The Australian Indigenous Governance Institute, Aurora Education Foundation and Country Needs People are three that immediately come to mind.

Learning and adapting

The biggest learning from the referendum is that we require new political strategies for Indigenous advancement. The politics of asking must cease. Many activists will want to hit the streets once again, but this is not the 1970s. The Sorry Day rally in 2000 and the School Strike 4 Climate rally in 2019, each of which brought many thousands of people to the streets, failed to move government. And the treatment of asylum seekers demonstrates Australia cares little for its international reputation.

What we need is a different kind of political action. This action will require support, membership, funding and clear communication, but never asking for permission.

We need innovation and imagination for this, and our allies must be brave and willing to step into these more radical spaces with us.

Perhaps most importantly, this renewed political action requires new leadership.

Passing the baton

The generations of Indigenous leaders who have steered our communities, and the campaign for constitutional recognition, deserve our deepest gratitude. It takes a certain type of person to take the hits and keep standing up and moving forward. To our leaders who have offered us strength and shone light on a righteous path, we will forever look up to you – 14 October will not be your legacy. A new generation of leaders has followed in your footsteps and grown up in your shadow. Now is the time to pass the baton of leadership.

That new generation is already here – and we are hungry for the opportunity. Hand us not the baton of defeat but strength in the struggle. May each 'yes' vote cast in the referendum be a drop of rain that nourishes the land as it seeks to heal itself.

With concerted effort, and sympathetic yet radical activism, 14 October may be remembered as the firestorm that tore through our nation, but from which green shoots of opportunity sprung.

In the 1800s, colonisers tried to listen to First Nations people, but it didn't stop the massacres

Stephen Gapps
University of Newcastle
Lynda-June Coe
Macquarie University

In a historic year when the nation voted on a referendum to enshrine an Aboriginal and Torres Strait Islander Voice to Parliament in the Constitution, it is worth considering the long history of how governments have tried and failed to authentically listen to First Nations people. And not just post-Federation governments. During Australia's colonial period in the 19th century, the office of the Protector of Aborigines was established in an effort to hear the 'wants, wishes and grievances' of Aboriginal people, as the secretary for the colonies, Lord Glenelg, put it in 1838. However, this office not only failed to genuinely listen to First Nations people, it led to policies that actually underpinned the erasure of Aboriginal and Torres Strait Islander people from the Australian Constitution of 1901.

Spotlight on the treatment of Indigenous people

In the early 1800s, a growing humanitarian movement in the United Kingdom had pushed the government to abolish slavery. By the 1830s, slave rebellions in Britain's colonies turned a spotlight on the treatment of Indigenous peoples, both within and on the edges of the rapidly expanding British Empire.

In 1836, the British Government established the Select Committee of the House of Commons on Aborigines to hear testimony from church leaders, missionaries and colonial officials about the situation concerning Aboriginal people in the Australian colonies. The hearings focused particular attention on the conduct of militia forces in the so-called Black War in Tasmania, where roving parties of white men hunted down and killed Palawa people, and massacres were seen as part and parcel of occupying Aboriginal lands.

In January 1838, Glenelg wrote to the governor of New South Wales, Sir George Gipps, that the British Government had 'directed their anxious attention to the adoption of some plan for the better protection and civilisation of the native tribes'. Glenelg told Gipps that, as part of the scheme, the British Government had decided to 'appoint a small number of persons qualified to fill the office of Protector of Aborigines'. The chief protector, a non-Indigenous person, was to be aided by four assistant protectors and 'fix his principal station at Port Phillip' (later to become Melbourne), only recently occupied by the British.

According to Glenelg, George Augustus Robinson was bestowed with the office of chief protector as he had 'shewn [sic] himself to be eminently qualified by his charge of the Aboriginal Establishment at Flinders Island'. Robinson's so-called 'Friendly Mission' – a series of journeys around Tasmania in the early 1830s intended to convince Palawa people of governor George Arthur's humane intentions – was lauded by Gipps as a success, as it had peacefully convinced some people to move to a reserve at Flinders Island. Historians now consider this mission to be nothing more than ethnic cleansing.

For Glenelg, appointing Robinson to the new position of chief protector appeared to be the only plan available that did not involve the military or police, or armed settlers dispensing their own 'justice'.

An aim to convey 'wants, wishes and grievances'

The plan for establishing Aboriginal protectorates followed Robinson's Friendly Mission model in Tasmania. Protectors were to 'watch over the rights and interests of the natives' and protect them from 'acts of cruelty, of oppression or injustice'. The protector was also to be a kind of conduit to express the 'wants, wishes and grievances' of Aboriginal people to the colonial governments. For this purpose, each protector was commissioned as a magistrate. Each protector was also encouraged to learn the 'language of the natives' and 'obtain accurate information' on the 'number of the natives within his district'.

On paper at least, the 'plan for the better protection and civilisation of the native tribes' seemed a remarkable step forward from previous years. Indeed, there was no plan prior to this that attempted to deal with the situation on Aboriginal lands beyond the official boundaries of the colonies – boundaries that were being increasingly crossed by hundreds of squatters and stockmen, and tens of thousands of cattle and sheep.

The establishment of the role of protectors, who would live among Aboriginal people and learn their languages, was arguably an early attempt at a mechanism for an Aboriginal voice to government.

A failure from the beginning

But the scheme did not stop the conflicts and massacres. In January and June 1838, shortly after the committee's report appeared in print in Australia, dozens of Gamilaraay people were killed at Waterloo Creek and Myall Creek in northern inland New South Wales. The scheme also did little to stop the resistance warfare that broke out across the entire length of the frontier in the late 1830s and early 1840s – a counteroffensive that has been described by some contemporary observers as a 'general uprising'.

The protectorates scheme was also bound up in the supposed superiority of the colonisers' race and Christian religion. The ultimate goal was for Aboriginal people to become 'civilised' and Christian – just like white people apparently were. It was a paternalistic concept that ultimately turned humanitarian ideals into an even more violent and coercive colonial system.

The protectors, as they had been directed to do, could report to the government the 'grievances' of Aboriginal people. As one observer at the time wrote, these were often found to be an 'explosion of long-pent feelings of revenge and hatred towards the whites, resulting from a long course of violence and injustice'. The attempt by the colonial authorities to understand the 'wants, wishes and grievances' of Aboriginal people, however, failed in its mission to actually protect people. The system was abandoned in 1849.

From the 1860s, the various colonial governments developed even more coercive policies of 'protection', which controlled people's lives and corralled them into missions and reserves, so their lands and children could be taken from them.

How this history feeds into failed policies today

The establishment of the office of the Protector of Aborigines was an important historical moment that embedded this idea of government control over First Nations people's lives into the social and political fabric of this nation. These supposedly moral standards around 'protection' and 'civilisation' ultimately forced Indigenous people to become less connected to their culture.

These beliefs continue to permeate our government today through failed paternalistic policies such as Closing the Gap. Such racialised policies draw on Australia's history of containment of Aboriginal land and the ongoing colonial violence of 'protection'. Because of this, we have yet to generate new possibilities for truly meaningful dialogue.

The long struggle for rights and recognition by Aboriginal people has been punctuated by (all too few) moments of support by non-Aboriginal people. With the referendum for the Voice, another such moment beckoned. History, unfortunately, repeated itself.

Long before the Voice vote, the Australian Aboriginal Progressive Association called for parliamentary representation

John Maynard
University of Newcastle

The most startling point about the referendum for a Voice to Parliament is the fact the majority of people in this country have no idea of history. And I mean both Black and white people.

Australian history, as written for nearly two-thirds of the 20th century, glorified discoverers, explorers, settlers and Gallipoli. We, as Aboriginal people, had been conveniently erased from the historical landscape and memory. Most Australians gave Aboriginal people little or no consideration. The majority of Aboriginal people were trapped in a historical vacuum through the fact that great numbers of our people had been confined to heavily congested and controlled missions and reserves.

As part of this confinement, we were encouraged to forget our past. Everyday decisions were removed from people; they were told what to eat, what to wear and who they could marry. Their movement was also severely restricted. There was a process of historical erasure and memory.

We were to be severed from any sense of past or inspiration. We could not participate in ceremonies, speak our language, tell our stories, practise songs and dances or conduct our everyday hunting and living experiences. Over time, our people could only remember the controlled life on the reserve. It became the pattern of misery.

In his 1968 Boyer lecture, 'After the Dreaming', anthropologist WEH Stanner exposed Australia's failure to regard, record or acknowledge Aboriginal people in the country's history. Australian history, he said, had been constructed with 'a view from a window which had been carefully placed to exclude a whole quadrant of the landscape'.

What is critically important in our understanding of history is that the call for a Voice to Parliament was not a new initiative. Aboriginal activists nearly 100 years ago first called for a Voice to Parliament as part of their political platform and demands during the 1920s.

The Australian Aboriginal Progressive Association

The first Aboriginal political organisation, the Australian Aboriginal Progressive Association (AAPA), was formed in Sydney in 1924 and led by my grandfather, Fred Maynard. It advocated several key demands to protect the rights of Aboriginal people, centring on:

- a national land rights agenda
- preventing Aboriginal children from being taken from their families
- a call for genuine Aboriginal self-determination
- citizenship in our own country
- defending a distinct Aboriginal cultural identity
- insisting Aboriginal people be placed in charge of Aboriginal affairs.

The call for Aboriginal rights to land was explicit. Leader Fred Maynard declared:

> The request made by this association for sufficient land for each eligible family is justly based. The Australian people are the original owners of the land and have a prior right over all other people in this respect.

The association's inaugural conference at St David's Church and Hall in Riley Street, Surry Hills was front-page news in Sydney's *Daily Guardian* – over 200 Aboriginal people attended. Within the space of six short months, the AAPA had expanded to thirteen branches, four sub-branches and a membership in excess of 600. Its established offices were on Crown Street, and it managed a statewide network of information regarding Aboriginal people.

Calls for direct representation in parliament

Late in October 1925, the association held a second conference in Kempsey, New South Wales. It ran over three days with over 700 Aboriginal people in attendance. It was noted in press coverage of the conference that 'pleas were entered for direct representation in parliament'.

Two years later, in 1927, the AAPA produced a manifesto. It was delivered to all sections of government – both state and federal – and published widely across New South Wales, South Australia, Victoria and Queensland. One of the significant points was for an Aboriginal board to be established under the Commonwealth Government, and for state control over Aboriginal lives to be abolished. It envisioned:

> The control of Aboriginal affairs, apart from common law rights shall be vested in a board of management comprised of capable educated Aboriginals under a chairman to be appointed by the government.

This board would not consist of government-selected or hand-picked individuals but Aboriginal-elected officers.

This push for an Aboriginal board or place in parliament continued in 1929, when Fred Maynard spoke to the Chatswood Willoughby Labour League in New South Wales on Aboriginal issues. A report in *The Labor Daily* newspaper in February that year mentioned his call for an:

> Aboriginal representative in the federal parliament, or failing it, to have an [A]boriginal ambassador appointed to live in Canberra to watch over his people's interests and advise the federal authorities.

Surveillance, threats, intimidation, abuse

The AAPA disappeared from public view in late 1929. There is strong evidence the organisation was effectively broken up through the combined efforts of the NSW Aborigines Protection Board, missionaries and the police. The state government and the Protection Board had been embarrassed by the exposure of their unjust policies in the media and wanted the organisation dismantled.

Fred Maynard, in an interview in late 1927 in *The Newcastle Sun*, revealed the level of surveillance, threat, intimidation and abuse he and the other Aboriginal activists were subjected to. The report noted:

> He said that he had been warned on many occasions that the doors of Long Bay were opening for him. He would cheerfully go to jail for the remainder of his life, he declared if, by so doing he could make the people of Australia realise the truly frightful administration of the Aborigines Act. He knew cases where children had been torn from their mothers and sent into absolute slavery.

When one ponders the legacy of the AAPA, the sad reality is that if the demands of these early activists had been met nearly a century ago, we would not be suffering the severe disadvantage that still hovers over Aboriginal lives today.

Imagine if enough land for each and every Aboriginal family to build their own economic independence had been granted.

Or that we would not have suffered another five decades of Aboriginal child removal and the shocking impact of that policy on generations of Aboriginal lives.

If the demand to protect a distinct Aboriginal cultural identity had been taken up, we would not today be working to repair the shattered cultural pieces of language, stories, songs and dances.

And finally, if Aboriginal people had been placed in a position to oversee Aboriginal policy and needs, the history of our people would have been vastly different.

The reality today is we continue to fight for the demands that the Australian Aboriginal Progressive Association established nearly 100 years ago.

PART II

On politics and war

Yes, Israel's occupation of Palestinian lands has to end, but massacres of civilians won't bring this end any closer

Eyal Mayroz
University of Sydney

Notwithstanding a brief period of hope in the mid-1990s, successive Israeli governments have long held that the country's security must inevitably rely on military might. But what may have worked in other places has not proven sustainable for the complex realities of the Israel–Palestine situation.

During the century-long feud between the two sides over land, there has been little respite from violence. Competing territorial claims continue to fuel duelling narratives of victimisation. These foment anger, animosity, fear and mistrust. Colossal leadership errors on both sides during historical junctures have led to missed opportunities to resolve a conflict that becomes more intractable by the year.

On the Jewish Israeli side, deep-rooted existential fears, following millennia of persecution, pogroms and the trauma of the Holocaust, were exacerbated by a number of mostly defensive wars fought against neighbouring Arab states. From the 1960s, Israel's desire for security was further challenged by continual terrorist attacks targeting its civilians. These experiences resulted in strong society-wide yearnings – to a level unfathomable by outsiders – for military supremacy as a means to ensure the country's survival.

On the Palestinian side, experiences of dispossession, injustice, deprivation, daily humiliation, endless violations of rights and a sense of abandonment by the world – including Arab states – have caused immeasurable despair.

Adding to the tensions since the 1980s have been the steadily increasing influences of religious and radical nationalist ideologies on both sides of the fence. These developments have all but stymied hopes for a negotiated end to the conflict in the foreseeable future.

Palestinian despair

After decades of oppression, the sense of hopelessness among Palestinians has reached a peak, aggravated by the realities on the ground:

- a continuing illegal expansion of Jewish settlements in the West Bank and fears of wholesale annexation of Palestinian lands

- worsening Jewish settler violence, aided at times, or at least not prevented, by Israel's security forces
- a suffocating sixteen-year blockade of Gaza since Israel's withdrawal from the strip, interspersed with bouts of violence between Israel and Hamas or Islamic Jihad, with civilians as the main victims
- diminishing prospects for an independent Palestinian state.

Consequently, 2023 has seen a significant rise in violent clashes between Israelis and Palestinians, mostly in the West Bank, but also in Gaza and inside Israel.

This was the situation on the eve of Hamas's horrendous attack on southern Israel on 7 October. The savage massacre of at least 1400 Israeli civilians, including whole families, women, children, babies and the elderly, in addition to the kidnapping of an estimated 200 more civilians, shocked the world. It brought an instantaneous Israeli declaration of war against Hamas.

Thousands of Palestinians were killed in the Israeli bombardments of the Gaza Strip that followed the attack – mostly civilians. Many thousands were wounded.

Little empathy across fences

Israeli historian Yuval Noah Harari has noted that while nations can become at once victims and perpetrators of violence, such situations can be psychologically difficult to cope with. Indeed, once we choose to support a side in a conflict, we may go to great lengths to defend its actions. New information, processed through our filters and conditioned responses, can be used to challenge, or cast doubt on, any claim made by the other side. The more emotionally invested we become in the cause, the harder it is for us to empathise with the suffering experienced across the fence.

At the start of this latest war, the heated debates and protests around the world demonstrated this 'empathy deficit' in action. On one side, many supporters of the pro-Palestinian camp, exasperated by the rapid increase in casualties and deteriorating conditions in Gaza, seemed reluctant to extend empathy to Israeli victims. Across the divide, traumatised supporters of Israel reacted furiously to any attempt to draw lines or parallels between the Hamas attack and Israel's mistreatment of Palestinians.

Saying 'no' to any violence against civilians

Supporters of a free Palestine have often been reluctant in the past to publicly criticise Hamas. For those who live in the Occupied Territories, fear may have been a factor. Another possible reason could have been the belief that disparaging groups like Hamas would undermine the cohesiveness and solidarity of their camp, and thus play into the hands of Israel.

A question for the Palestinians to ask themselves, though, is whether the campaign is inflicting greater damage on its cause, both morally and practically, by not distancing itself more categorically from violent groups like Hamas and Islamic Jihad who target civilians. This question seems all the more relevant in the aftermath of 7 October.

By provoking Israel and hiding behind its own civilian population, using them as human shields – with full knowledge of what Israel's response would be – Hamas demonstrated a willingness to sacrifice thousands of Gazans in the hope of raising the world's anger against Israel. This highly immoral and cruel strategy seems to have worked only partially – at least in the initial days of the war.

Ending the occupation

Decades of Israeli occupation of the Palestinian territories, meanwhile, have inflicted immeasurable hurt and suffering on the Palestinian people. The occupation has also caused significant damage to Israel's social fabric, cohesion, economy, international standing, security, moral stature and more. The occupation should end, and the sooner the better. The question is how. The challenges, already vexing before Hamas's attack, have now become much greater. Would Israelis be willing to risk having a Hamas-run Palestinian state not just in Gaza but potentially in the West Bank as well one day, just 10 kilometres from Tel Aviv?

Many foreign governments have been formulating their policies on the conflict with the aim of minimising potential harm to their diplomatic, geostrategic and economic interests. The world has lost hope in the viability of the proposed solutions currently on the table. Global attention is also short. As soon as one cycle of violence ends, the world's focus will drift away from Israel–Palestine to the next crisis.

Many Western countries, including Australia, continue to profess support for the Palestinians' right to a state, but without formally recognising such a state. This recognition, the argument goes, should be made as part of negotiations over a two-state solution – one for Israelis and the other for Palestinians. However, as meaningful negotiations have not been carried out for years, how helpful, really, is such a policy for advancing a resolution to the conflict? Recognition of West Jerusalem as Israel's capital could and should go hand in hand with formal recognition of a Palestinian state, with East Jerusalem as its capital.

Perhaps the concern and passion currently being manifested by supporters of the two sides could lead this time to more effective action. Those who care about Palestine should denounce terror, cruelty and violence against civilians, and put more pressure on their governments to support an end to the Israeli occupation in return for more viable solutions for Israel's legitimate security needs. Those who are concerned about Israel should do the same.

There are no easy solutions to this conflict, but military ones won't do anymore. Violence only begets more violence. It has to stop.

New Zealand's new Prime Minister defeated the left at the 2023 election, but his real test lies to his right

Richard Shaw
Massey University

Christopher Luxon is no slouch on the dance floor, it seems. As his wife, Amanda, told the *New Zealand Woman's Weekly*, the two prepared for their university ball with a ballroom dancing class: 'The teacher said he had rhythm and I couldn't believe she was saying that about him when I had done ballet for years. But that's what clinched it for me!' As the pace increased in the campaign for New Zealand's 2023 general election – and regardless of polls showing the National Party ahead of Labour – Luxon needed to find some of that rhythm both in the weeks leading up to and after the election.

As an unimpressive TV performance defending his party's tax package demonstrated during the campaign, he'll need stamina and skill to make up for being a comparative newcomer to the political dance. But this became even more important after the election because the landscape on the right of New Zealand politics is changing. In particular, ACT New Zealand's success in stitching together a coalition of urban, low-tax-loving liberals and disaffected farmers is driving a wedge between the National Party and the voters it has long seen as its own.

Luxon's party faced not just an election but a generational realignment. Rebranding an airline, as Luxon did in a former life, is one thing. Steering the National Party through what lies ahead may require more than fancy footwork.

The political unknown

This is no small task for a political novice. Luxon only entered parliament as the MP for Botany at the 2020 election. National lost the party vote to Labour in that Auckland constituency, and the 50 per cent of the candidate vote he gained was lower than the 60 per cent that National's Jami-Lee Ross won in 2017.

If it was a baptism by fire, he fared better than a lot of National's other candidates in that election, which gave Labour the first single-party majority government since the adoption of the mixed-member proportional electoral system in 1996. That seismic defeat saw the end of Judith Collins's leadership and the search for a new face. A little over a year later, Luxon was installed as the party's fifth leader in just four years.

It's been less than two years since then, but much has changed. Most notably, former prime minister Jacinda Ardern has gone – as have all of the COVID-19 restrictions and many of the policies with which she was associated. During that time, Luxon worked hard to construct a political persona, but he routinely faced claims he was an unknown quantity.

His previous careers at Unilever and Air New Zealand are well known, as is the fact he's a conservative Christian. Some might know he likes waterskiing and country music. Some may even rate his credentials on the climate crisis, gender pay equity and his opposition to human trafficking. Yet Luxon still lacks political definition in a way John Key – the former National leader and prime minister, whose political success it is Luxon's job to reprise – did not.

The two things most people knew about Key were that he was born in a state house (public housing) and grew up to become an international man of finance. The first fact allowed Key to promote himself as an ordinary bloke, the second notwithstanding. Luxon – who earned NZ$4.4 million a year at Air New Zealand and owns seven houses – has yet to pull off that political sleight of hand.

Brand Luxon

Earlier in the campaign, that slight sense of fuzziness – the feeling that people are not quite sure who Luxon is or what he stands for – was a concern for National's strategists, forcing them to distinguish the leader from the party on the campaign trail. There were worries, too, about the gap between Luxon's personal polling and those of prime minister Chris Hipkins (and, for different reasons, those of ACT leader David Seymour). However, the head-to-head contest for preferred prime minister between Luxon and Hipkins tightened considerably as the campaign wore on.

But concerns about the extent to which 'brand Luxon' was achieving cut-through with voters did not entirely go away. For one thing, the same poll that had Luxon just a couple of percentage points behind Hipkins as preferred prime minister suggested he was less popular among undecided voters, who often determine the outcome of elections. Furthermore, in another pre-election poll, only 25 per cent of women respondents felt well disposed towards Luxon, whereas 39 per cent expressed some degree of negativity towards him, which may speak to his socially conservative views on (among other things) abortion.

In 2020, National lost significant support among women to Ardern. It needed those votes back if it was to prevail this time, which goes some way to explaining the composition of National's party list – even if Luxon was less than keen to acknowledge gender was a factor in drawing it up.

A busy dance card

It is worth recalling, however, that before the 2020 election, National's figures were in freefall. Luxon turned that around, calming a querulous caucus and ending National's leadership musical chairs. He also made sure the party's list more closely resembles the wider population, with fewer middle-aged white males per capita than previously.

That said, reflecting on the views held by a number of those on that list, one journalist suggested a National victory could produce 'an unruly rump of zealots championing Christian identity politics' and pose 'a significant risk to National's cohesiveness and its ability to hold that power'.

But unlike Ardern in 2020, Luxon will not be dancing with himself as leader of the next government. As head of a delicate coalition arrangement, this may be where the skills developed in his previous careers will be most severely tested.

ACT's own experience in office is limited to Seymour's brief tenure – a decade ago – as Minister of Regulatory Reform and parliamentary undersecretary to the Minister of Education. And some of its candidate selections raise concerns about the sorts of views held within a party that's now part of a government.

A resurgent New Zealand First also poses a threat. These days it is as much a populist party seeking to 'take the country back' from sundry 'elites' and 'a small unelected cabal of opinionated virtue signallers' as it is a vehicle for economic nationalism.

Both ACT and NZ First ended up on Luxon's dance card once the votes were counted. Now he just has to avoid tripping over his own feet as the real business of government begins.

Author, ambassador, commentator, critic? It's not always easy to earn a crust as a former PM

Frank Bongiorno
Australian National University

Few Australians are losing sleep over how former prime minister Scott Morrison is going to earn a crust after politics. Few outside the federal Coalition, at any rate. His continuing presence on the Opposition backbench following the Coalition's 2022 election loss has served as a distraction from the present and a reminder of the past.

Morrison's prime ministership was a landmark in one respect that is rarely noticed. Leaving aside the independently wealthy Malcolm Turnbull, Morrison is the first prime minister originally elected to parliament under the post-2004 superannuation arrangements for politicians. These were the result of a decision made by the Howard government, as a defensive measure against an insurgent Labor Party under Mark Latham, to end the gold-plated scheme that had politicians getting a pension for life once they had been in parliament for eight years, with further generous benefits for ministers.

Of course, former prime ministers receive many other goodies, such as office facilities and free travel, but that does not earn them a living. Morrison is just fifty-five, with a young family. He does not seem short of a quid, but it is easy to see why he might be reluctant to surrender his parliamentary salary without having something else lined up.

He has been shopping himself around and seems to imagine a future on the lecture circuit. That is potentially a nice little earner for an ex-leader, as Tony Blair and Bill Clinton have shown. But as US vice-presidential candidate senator Lloyd Bentsen might have put it if he were still around: 'Scott, you're no Bill Clinton.' The opportunities for this former Australian prime minister to play wise elder statesman seem unpromising.

Clinton, like all former US presidents, remains 'Mr President', but it is different under a parliamentary system. There is no obvious role for a former Australian prime minister to play. Nor is there an obvious career path for them to take to keep themselves in the manner that they presumably see as befitting their status. If you are wealthy, like Turnbull or Kevin Rudd, there is nothing to worry about. But matters are more complicated for others. Even Robert Menzies relied on benefactors to help him acquire a home in Melbourne after spending sixteen years in The Lodge.

So, what have our ex-prime ministers done with their post–prime ministerial lives? Five never had to face the dilemma. Joseph Lyons and John Curtin died in office, and Harold Holt disappeared at sea. Ben Chifley died as Opposition leader in 1951, after losing an election to Menzies in December 1949. Alfred Deakin tragically lost his mind.

Edmund Barton, our first, went to the High Court, but he is unique in following that course. Several have assumed diplomatic appointments. High commissioner in London was popular in the early decades of last century, and a natural progression given that prime ministers, not external affairs or foreign ministers, had primary responsibility for relations with the United Kingdom.

George Reid, Andrew Fisher, Joseph Cook and Stanley Melbourne Bruce all took on this role. Reid subsequently entered the House of

Commons for the Conservative Party for a brief period before his death. Bruce distinguished himself as high commissioner for over a decade, taking in the latter years of the Depression and World War II before he went to the House of Lords as Viscount Bruce of Melbourne. The practice of sending ex-prime ministers on major diplomatic postings then fell into disuse. The Hawke government appointed Gough Whitlam to Paris as ambassador to the United Nations Educational, Scientific and Cultural Organization (UNESCO), but Rudd's March 2023 appointment to Washington is otherwise a departure from patterns established since World War II.

Efforts to gain a prestigious international role have usually produced disappointment. Malcolm Fraser failed in a bid to become secretary-general of the Commonwealth, but he did serve on the eminent persons group trying to end apartheid in South Africa and chaired the international relief agency CARE Australia. The even more exalted role of secretary-general of the United Nations (UN) eluded Rudd.

Others have tried business. Bob Hawke biographer Troy Bramston reports that he 'made a lot of money in the 1990s and 2000s', with China a focus. Hawke had excellent business connections stretching back to his time at the Australian Council of Trade Unions, and made the most of them. In general, his business activities, combined with criticisms of his successor Paul Keating, did little to restore his reputation. Keating himself pursued business opportunities, taking an interest in Sydney planning issues, and has now emerged as the harshest public critic of AUKUS.

Most write memoirs, which can be lucrative. Menzies, Whitlam, Hawke, John Howard, Julia Gillard and Turnbull did well with sales; Rudd less so. Fraser also wrote books as he became more critical of the Liberal Party he once led. Howard and Gillard have continued to write, while Gillard was a founder and remains chair of the Global Institute for Women's Leadership, established at King's College London and now also based at the Australian National University (ANU); she has interested herself in girls' education. Whitlam was a visiting fellow at the ANU for a time after politics.

The problem for ex-prime ministers today is that the dynamics of political careers have changed. Politics was once essentially a profession; now, it is more commonly a stage in a career and those leaving the job are often only in their fifties.

Billy Hughes was for a time Australia's longest-serving prime minister, in the role from late 1915 through to early 1923. But these were just a few years in a political career that stretched from his election to the NSW Parliament as an early Labor member in 1894, to serving in the House of Representatives with several parties from 1901 through to his death in 1952. Another Billy, McMahon, continued in parliament for almost a decade after his defeat at the 1972 election, offering commentary on his own side of politics that was rarely cherished.

Ironically, the greatest harm McMahon did to his party after 1972 was an ill-timed resignation that saw his seat of Lowe go to Labor. But when prime ministers deposed by their own side have stayed on – Hughes, John Gorton, Rudd and Tony Abbott – they can do their successors a little or a lot of damage.

Gorton appeared in a whisky ad, and Whitlam advertised pasta sauce and telephones. Morrison made his career in marketing and gained a public profile over the controversial 'Where the bloody hell are you?' Australian tourism campaign.

A master spruiker, perhaps the answer to Morrison's dilemma lies under his nose.

Who needs PwC when consultancy work could be done more efficiently in-house?

Emmanuel Josserand
University of Technology Sydney

The PricewaterhouseCoopers (PwC) scandal prompted a Senate inquiry into consulting firms this year, as well as an inquiry by the NSW Legislative Council into the state government's use of management consulting services. While the PwC case highlights confidentiality risks and conflicts of interests, the Legislative Council inquiry targets a potential lack of value for money and the negative impact on the capability development of the public service.

As consulting expenditure by government has risen globally, so have questions about the efficiency of such expenditures. 'Do-it-yourself' (DIY) consulting – the creation of internal consulting teams within the public service – can contribute to reducing consulting costs while futureproofing public service management.

Debates on the negative impact of consulting on the public service rage in the United States, United Kingdom and Europe. French President Emmanuel Macron faced severe criticism during his presidential campaign regarding the use of consultants by his government. In Australia, the costs from the big four consulting firms (Deloitte, KPMG, PwC and Ernst & Young) increased by more than 400 per cent in the 2012–22 period, leading to a national controversy.

The Albanese government pledged to reduce consulting costs dramatically and has begun to do so, with a reduction of around one-third in consulting expenditure in 2023. But now that it has picked the low-hanging fruit, what comes next?

Do we actually need external consultants?

Management consulting firms sell themselves by spruiking that they provide specialised advice on complex issues, and temporary resources to accelerate change resulting in increased performance. When it comes to backing these claims, there is ample anecdotal evidence but very little substantiating data.

There is limited proof of the positive impact of external management consulting on private companies' performance. However, the evidence is almost non-existent in the public service. More alarmingly, there is emerging evidence of a negative impact. A study conducted over six years on 125 hospitals in the United Kingdom concludes:

> If the average annual expenditure on consulting services for a hospital trust is considered (around £1.2 million), then each one would be roughly £10,600 worse off per annum (in addition to the consulting fees paid).

Research also shows that decision-makers and consulting firms generally only assess the impact of consulting projects through subjective measures or not at all. In the absence of hard evidence, this is likely to sanction further use with no real scrutiny.

Adding to this anecdotal assessment is the reality that consultants (particularly the big four) are very good at PR, sales and exploiting the pressure on executive performance to create an addiction whereby consulting begets more consulting. Their networks become embedded in those of senior public servants, also providing a lucrative future career option for those who leave the public service.

While there is a case to be made for some use of external management consulting, this should be restricted to temporary situations or situations in which very specific expertise can't be sourced elsewhere. So, yes, there is a role for consultants in the public service, but certainly a much more modest one.

Doing more internally

Public and private organisations, including the World Bank, the Australian Taxation Office, the Australian Department of Health, Telstra and National Australia Bank, have dedicated departments or internal consulting teams that, on a daily basis, conduct the types of activities that can be outsourced to consultants. Such teams deliver internally similar services to those that can be expected from management consultants. These include strategic planning, strategic project management, change management and digitisation initiatives.

The new Australian Centre for Evaluation, focused on evaluating key government programs across the federal government, is a good (if small) start. While not all services can be managed internally, internal consulting teams could deliver a much broader range of benefits for federal and state governments.

The first obvious benefit, in light of the PwC scandal, is confidentiality. Public servants don't have the type of conflict of interest that consultants have. They don't face the same choices between the interests of their different clients, between their own interests and those of their clients, or between their ethics and their financial objectives.

DIY consulting can also significantly reduce costs. Recent research shows that the more management teams are involved in internal consulting, the less the consulting costs. There is thus the potential for substituting expensive outsourced work with less costly internal teams. Over time, such savings should offset the establishment costs of internal teams.

DIY consulting can also contribute to futureproofing the public service. One of the dangers of relying heavily on management consultants is that it results in a 'hollowing out', a process by which the public service progressively loses skills. Creating internal consulting teams counters this by providing opportunities to rebuild skills and capabilities. This is especially important at a time when artificial intelligence (AI) and automation will potentially endanger jobs or, at the very least, change the skills needed across the economy, including the public sector.

The recent outcry against management consultants in the public sphere has not been matched by an outpouring of ideas on how to change the situation. Governments have become so addicted to consultants that cutting them off cold turkey is not necessarily a workable solution given the skills and knowledge gaps that have been created. DIY consulting may just be a way for the public sector to weather the withdrawal symptoms and finally wean itself off its consultancy dependence.

What should the Australian War Memorial do with its heroic portraits of Ben Roberts-Smith?

Kit Messham-Muir
Curtin University

Earlier this year, the Federal Court dismissed Ben Roberts-Smith's defamation case against *The Age*, *The Sydney Morning Herald* and *The Canberra Times*. Justice Anthony Besanko ruled the newspapers had established, by the 'balance of probabilities' (the standard of evidence in a civil lawsuit), that Roberts-Smith had committed war crimes.

Following the ruling, much public debate focused on what the Australian War Memorial should do with Roberts-Smith's uniform, helmet and other artefacts of his on display.

In September, the memorial added a revised text panel to the display that acknowledged the findings of the defamation case and the ongoing legal process. Roberts-Smith is appealing the ruling.

Greens senator David Shoebridge, however, has called for the removal of these objects from public display to correct the official record and 'to begin telling the entire truth of Australia's involvement in that brutal war'.

So, what should the war memorial do? Should the display be removed, effectively cancelled, or changed to tell the full story?

The case of the oil paintings

It is not just these artefacts on display. The memorial also has two heroic oil-painting portraits of Roberts-Smith by one of Australia's leading artists, Michael Zavros, which it commissioned in 2014. *Pistol Grip (Ben Roberts-Smith VC)* is a larger-than-life-sized depiction of Roberts-Smith, camouflaged arms outstretched, mimicking the action of holding a pistol. The smaller *Ben Roberts-Smith VC* depicts him in ceremonial military uniform.

In an article for the arts criticism website Memo, respected Monash University art historian Rex Butler and arts journalist Paris Lettau weighed into the debate. Butler and Lettau say *Pistol Grip* is 'threatening, over-bearing, macho, hyper-masculine, celebratory and enormous, like the man himself – some 220 centimetres wide and 160 centimetres high'.

When Zavros created his large portrait, it was a depiction of a soldier doing what he was trained to do – and venerated for doing. It is an aggressive pose that, given current developments, can be read in a much more sinister way.

This all touches on the far bigger question of how national institutions for the public memory of war address difficult and morally ambiguous moments in a national story.

Moral and ethical ambiguity

When the Canadian War Museum opened at its new site in Ottawa in 2005, its displays included two paintings by Canadian artist Gertrude Kearns. The paintings, *Somalia without Conscience* (1996) and *The Dilemma of Kyle Brown: Paradox in the Beyond* (1995), deal with one of the most shameful episodes in Canada's military history, known as the Somalia Affair.

In 1992, the Canadian Airborne Regiment was deployed as peacekeepers to Somalia. In 1993, sixteen-year-old Shidane Arone was found hiding in the Canadian base, and was believed to have been stealing supplies. He was tortured, and soldiers photographed themselves with the semiconscious boy. Master corporal Clayton Matchee and his subordinate private Kyle Brown were charged with his torture and murder.

Somalia without Conscience depicts Matchee posing with the beaten Arone, while *The Dilemma of Kyle Brown* depicts Brown symbolically holding two potential fates in his hands: a lightly coloured cube in his right hand and a darkened cube in his left. It addresses an ethical grey area many soldiers face during active service, when the hierarchy of command comes into direct conflict with conscience.

Following the opening of the new Canadian War Museum, the presence of Kearns's paintings sparked intense debate. Curator Laura Brandon received abusive emails from members of the public. The museum also copped criticism from figures such as the head of the National Council of Veterans Associations, who called the paintings a 'trashy, insulting tribute' and urged a boycott of the museum.

Discussing this controversy in 2007, Brandon said what upset veteran communities was that 'their' museum 'was not only telling the stories of heroism and courage that most of them expected to be told but also stories about failures, disappointments, and human frailty'. Brandon remained steadfast in believing the museum needed to address the messy ambiguities of war and, despite pressure, kept Kearns's paintings on display for the duration of the exhibition.

The complexity of contemporary art

Brandon's curatorial decision to display Kearns's Somalia paintings strikes at the heart of what is special and important about contemporary war art in a national museum.

Contemporary art presents ethical and moral complexity, grey zones and a range of perspectives. This is vital in a healthy liberal democracy. While Brandon's choice to show Kearns's Somalia paintings attracted criticism, the museum remained committed to telling a story that is difficult, ethically and morally complex, and uncomfortable for Canadians.

To remove Zavros's portraits from display would remove the now-untenable hero narrative that once surrounded Roberts-Smith. But doing so would also rewrite public memory by effectively erasing an important part of why and how Roberts-Smith was revered.

These portraits now represent a morally complex story that needs to be addressed by our national war museum. To remove them would miss a valuable opportunity to debate important questions about how we construct hero stories.

So, how could these portraits still be shown in the future?

Zavros's portraits were already complex works before the ruling in the Roberts-Smith defamation case. In the wake of that ruling, it is important they are seen in all their additional multilayered and problematic complexity.

The portraits show us how we create the nation through the stories we tell ourselves, and how dynamic that narrative can be. These portraits present a valuable opportunity to show how narratives of war – like the stories of our own lives – are never simple, consistent and coherent.

The portraits should be displayed in ways that address this complexity, with the evolving story of Roberts-Smith captured in explanatory wall text. There is an opportunity here to not simply 'correct' the official record, as Shoebridge suggests, but to have a deeper conversation about the role of hero narratives in diverting attention away from more important public debates about Australia's involvements in conflicts. Maybe this could be addressed in the art the Australian War Memorial commissions in the future.

The most compelling contemporary artworks – and the most valuable displays in our national institutions – are those that consider our complex stories, raise important and self-reflective questions, and challenge simplistic narratives.

Editor's note: The article was amended post-publication to include the war memorial adding context about the defamation case to its display.

More corrupt, fractured and ostracised: How Vladimir Putin has changed Russia in over two decades on top

Matthew Sussex
Australian National University

Vladimir Putin's own version of history casts himself as modern Russia's bulwark and champion. According to this narrative, Putin has sturdily held back waves of foreign and domestic adversaries, and simultaneously restored Russia to greatness. But although these breathless tales of Putin's heroics may still resonate among Russians who've been spoonfed a rich diet of disinformation for years, informed observers will view them on a spectrum ranging from embellished to the absurd.

Future historians are unlikely to treat Putin kindly. He has ruled through a combination of fear and favour, cynically up-ending Russia's proto-democracy by making dissent a crime rather than a crucial part of political life. Russia has become a nation under the thrall of Putin's singular idea, instead of a healthy contest between competing ones.

He has progressively sickened Russian society, creating a toxic culture that celebrates xenophobia, nativism and violence.

And by launching a foolish war of imperial expansion in Ukraine that his much-vaunted modernised military has proved incapable of winning, he has inadvertently revealed the fragility of his own power structure.

Putin's ascent

Putin's political ascent began once he took over as head of the Russian Security Council in March 1999, long seen as a likely pathway to executive leadership. He then assumed Russia's prime ministership and, soon after, its presidency, as an increasingly infirm Boris Yeltsin sought to anoint a successor. Putin's willingness to protect the interests of 'the family' – the network of cronies and oligarchs comprising Yeltsin's inner circle – made him an obscure but nonetheless logical choice.

A struggle for order and stability has been a consistent leitmotif in how Putin has portrayed himself. He played up this theme during Russia's presidential election in 2000, which followed the crippling 1998 Russian financial crisis, and was held amid Russia's second war in Chechnya. In his debut campaign, Putin offered little beyond a vague promise to restore order and make Russia a great power again. He faced little opposition once two leading political figures – Moscow mayor Yuri Luzhkov and former prime minister Yevgeny Primakov – pulled out of the race. Russians elected him with 53 per cent of the vote, more out of a sense of relief than enthusiasm.

Upon assuming the leadership, Putin set about stabilising the economy. He amended Russia's tax code, replacing an arcane system of loopholes and tax breaks with flat rates to boost compliance. In 2004, he effectively renationalised the oil and gas industries after the forced break-up of Yukos, which controlled around 20 per cent of Russia's oil production.

This sent both an economic and a political message: Russia's future prosperity would be driven by energy revenues, and Russia's oligarchs would only prosper at Putin's pleasure. Such has been Russia's reliance on energy that, by 2021, taxes and dividends from oil and gas companies accounted for 45 per cent of Russia's federal budget.

Putin's economic miracle?

After the attacks on September 11, 2001 and the subsequent US-led global war on terror, Russia's economy rebounded, aided by high energy prices. Between 2000 and 2007, average disposable income increased considerably. Inflation fell and the economy grew by around 7 per cent a year, although real wages declined. While the economy suffered a recession as a result of the global financial crisis in 2008, growth was swiftly restored.

Annual household income rose to an estimated US$10,000 per capita in 2013, but by 2022 it had contracted to only US$7900. Hence, Russians have, on average, been worse off over the last decade. This is partly due to Western sanctions imposed after the country's annexation of Crimea in 2014. Following the 2022 invasion of Ukraine, Russia defaulted on its foreign currency debt (for the first time since 1918), and the economy entered recession in November that year.

Significant structural problems in Russia's economy and society have persisted under Putin. Wealth is unevenly distributed, concentrated in Moscow and St Petersburg, and in Russia's regions it's centred on local elites. Russian life expectancy under Putin has improved only slightly – in 2021, it was estimated at sixty-nine years, compared to sixty-five years in 2000. On average, Russians have shorter lives than Iraqis (seventy years) and only live marginally longer than citizens of Eritrea (sixty-seven years) and Ethiopia (sixty-five years).

Kleptocrats, meet autocrats

Bribery and institutionalised corruption have been just as much of a hallmark of Putin's rule as his predecessor's. Despite fanfare about clearing out the oligarchs, Russia has scored consistently poorly on Transparency International's Corruption Perceptions Index. In 2022, Russia was ranked 137th out of 180 nations. By comparison, after Putin had finished his first term as president in 2004, Russia placed ninetieth.

Putin's rule is also the story of Russia's slide from a 'managed' democracy to an autocratic regime. This was a gradual process, justified by the need for new laws to protect society.

It began in 2003 when Russian media were barred from political analysis during elections. By 2012, Putin's imposition of new laws that criminalised foreign agents, protests and criticism of the government saw Russia ranked 148th out of 176 countries on the Reporters Without

Borders Press Freedom Index. This year, it has slipped to 164th out of 180 countries.

Since the Ukraine invasion, Russians convicted of 'discrediting the military' have faced jail terms, fines, beatings, social ostracism, loss of income and benefits, and even psychiatric confinement.

Putin's legacy: Ostracism and fragility

Putin's Russia is a society in which enemies abound. With respect to perceived external adversaries – North Atlantic Treaty Organization (NATO) members and the broader West – Putin sees regime security as being synonymous with national security. As a result, his primary fears are personal, not geopolitical. It's not NATO expansion that concerns Putin, but what an alliance of largely democratic nations may bring with it: the prospect of 'colour revolutions', in which populations seek to wrest control from the hands of corrupt dictators.

By invading Ukraine, Putin has actually succeeded in enlarging NATO further, with Finland and Sweden joining the alliance. He has prompted Germany and other overdependent European states to wean themselves off Russian oil and gas. And he's ensured Russia will remain a Western pariah for the foreseeable future, while bequeathing Russia's next generation the lasting hatred of Ukrainians.

Russia now faces an uncertain future. Instead of Putin's vision of a Euro-Pacific great power, it seems destined to be little more than a nuclear-armed raw materials appendage of China. Even worse for Putin, his rule now looks increasingly tenuous. His failures in Ukraine have proven impossible for Russia's compliant state media to fashion into a story of triumph.

Putin's initial response to Yevgeny Prigozhin's dramatic mutiny in June 2023 added to the perception of weakness. It initially took him several hours to appear in an emergency broadcast, in which he spoke of a potential civil war and promised to liquidate the Wagner traitors. But only hours later, once a hasty deal with Prigozhin had been struck, that strong statement was walked back by Putin's press secretary, who was forced to paint the Wagner forces simultaneously as both heroes and enemies of the state.

Later, in an address to Russian soldiers, Putin thanked the military for saving Russia, even though it hadn't confronted the revolt.

The equally apathetic response by the general public (indeed, nobody tried to lie down in front of a Wagner tank to protect Putin) was also telling. So, too, was the fact that Wagner operatives were seemingly able to escape the mutiny unpunished, while ordinary citizens face jail terms for even short, silent protests.

Putin's Russia is starting to look like tsarist Russia: a state that collapsed under the weight of its own contradictions, as British historian Orlando Figes put it. Russia in 2023 now looks even more fractured than it did when Putin took over, ostensibly to save it from turmoil.

Perhaps the greatest irony of Putin's near-quarter-century at the helm, then, is that he has come to personify the chaos he has long professed to abhor.

Editor's note: Yevgeny Prigozhin and another Wagner commander were killed in a plane crash in Russia after the publication of this story.

Why 'wokeness' has become the latest battlefront for white conservatives in America

Emma Shortis
RMIT University
Liam Byrne
University of Melbourne

The day he launched his bid for the Republican nomination for the 2024 US presidential election, Florida governor Ron DeSantis warned *Fox News* viewers 'the woke mind virus is basically a form of cultural Marxism'. With his trademark subtlety, DeSantis was pitching himself to the Republican base that still supports Donald Trump, the current front-runner for the nomination.

For those in the know, it was a signal. With a President DeSantis, there would be no more critical race theory. There would be fewer protections for LGBTQIA+ people. And there would be no more troubling ambiguity in textbooks or any suggestion the United States is anything other than the greatest country on Earth, and always has been, and is going to be made great again. Or even greater.

Welcome to the War on Woke.

On *Fox*, DeSantis was trying to claim that he, not Trump, is the leading general in this war. But he is far from alone. Across the country, Republican-led state legislatures are unleashing a tidal wave of laws intended to enforce white conservative mores on the broader population. The War on Woke has involved brazen attacks on academic freedom in universities and schools; on the rights of transgender people, particularly children, to gender-affirming health care; and on any person, group or business deemed too liberal – even Mickey Mouse.

These shifting battlefronts are underpinned by a concerted effort to erase any form of American history that considers the racism and inequity of the country's past and present. The teaching of 'critical race theory' is being banned in many states, 'divisive concepts' are no longer allowed in school curricula, and any history that explores inequality is being expunged from school textbooks.

But although it may seem it, this War on Woke is not new.

In the 1950s, William Faulkner, the American novelist whose Southern Gothic fiction was haunted by the legacy of slavery, wrote: 'The past is never dead. It's not even past.' Zealous conservatives have banned Faulkner's books from school curricula on multiple occasions for obscenity and blasphemy.

Today's 'war' is part of a much longer fight – one that has dominated America's past, and continues to shape the possibilities of its future.

What is the War on Woke?

In Iowa earlier this year, Trump lamented the constant repetition of 'woke, woke, woke', complaining that 'it's just a term they use. Half the people can't define it; they don't know what it is.' As he so often does, Trump inadvertently highlighted the confounding and contradictory nature of American politics today.

The term 'woke' can be either an insult or a marker of pride – it can shift depending on the context. Both those broadly aligned with woke aims and those in bitter opposition to them appear to find it equally difficult to define the term.

As the journalist and author Michael Harriot has explained, the term 'woke' emerged from the African American maxim 'stay woke'; that is, a call to stay aware of the lived reality of racism in the United States.

More recently, the meaning has drifted and now signifies a broad commitment to social justice awareness and activism. It's not surprising, then, that it has drawn the opprobrium of a conservative right that is obsessed with entrenching its moral code as not just the dominant ethic but the law of the land.

So how do conservatives define wokeness and articulate the terms of their opposition? The simple answer is they don't. Many conservatives instead compare wokeness with a sickness, which is a way of associating those seeking to ameliorate social injustices with degradation, decay and moral turpitude.

The slippery nature of the term 'woke' is useful to those wishing to prosecute a war against anything that strays outside the rigid confines of conservative ideology. Its adaptability and malleability are crucial to its pervasiveness.

From civil war to civil rights

But this is hardly the first time in American history that states have passed regressive laws seeking to wind back social gains made at the federal level. The United States has never been one country. The dispersed, state-level battlefronts of the War on Woke reflect this historical reality.

The country was born as an uneasy alliance of settler colonies based on imperial expansion and dispossession. The white establishment in both the north and the south benefited from slavery, but there was a crucial difference: the south's entire economic foundation and social structure was built on it; the north's was not. This created a fundamental tension between the two social systems that, in the mid-19th century, erupted into outright conflict.

Depicting themselves as the victims of northern aggression, white southerners insisted they were simply seeking to protect their way of life. This meant not just the maintenance of slavery but its expansion. The 'carpetbaggers' from the north, meanwhile, were imposing an unjust and unwanted way of life on the south. This was a cultural construction that would endure long after the Civil War.

After losing the war, white southern leaders found new ways to assert power, through Jim Crow laws and the continued brutal oppression of African Americans and other racial minorities. In the 1960s, the civil rights movement began to challenge these discriminatory laws.

The backlash was swift. And it was, again, about a white minority population seeking to utilise the unequal mechanisms of the American constitutional order to maintain their authority. Loudly proclaiming 'states rights', they inveighed against the white northern elites once again interfering, so they alleged, with their way of life.

Conservatism was cohering into a new social movement, premised on the rejection of the advances of the civil rights movement. Its adherents despised all those they perceived as a threat to the social order they sought to (re)create: mobilised African Americans, feminists, lesbians and gays, migrants, and anybody else who could be broadly described as 'liberal'.

A new social movement is born

In a 1964 speech supporting the presidential campaign of Republican Barry Goldwater, Ronald Reagan, a rising star in the Republican Party, gave voice to these emerging politics:

> This is the issue of this election: Whether we believe in our capacity for self-government or whether we abandon the American revolution and confess that a little intellectual elite in a far-distant capital can plan our lives for us better than we can plan them ourselves.

Generations of free marketeers proudly repeat Reagan's words. What they neglect to mention is this was not a simple appeal for hearty and virtuous Americans to draw on their own resources and dictate their destinies, rather than rely on ineffective government bureaucracy. In the climate of the civil rights movement, it was a repetition of the racially coded southern call to assert the right to local self-government over interference from the central government, which was daring to support aspirations for genuine racial equality.

This was the culture war of the time. Conservatives mobilised in presidential campaigns, in student groups such as the Young Americans for Freedom, and in more insidious places, such as the John Birch Society and the Ku Klux Klan. Most significant of all was the organisation in churches, as a new, white, Christian evangelical movement discovered and embraced its power.

Reagan sought to identify himself with this conservative social movement sweeping the country, against the Republican establishment of the day. The tactic elevated him to the governorship of California and, later, the White House.

This right-wing mobilisation included a forceful campaign against educational materials provided by the government to school students that sought to capture the complexities of American history. Conservative Christians also campaigned against depictions of Black oppression and assertions of non-white culture, sex education, and anything else that might challenge their carefully prescribed social code.

The past is never dead

The War on Woke is the most recent incarnation of this ongoing culture war. It is a means of mobilisation, but also of cultural definition. By being against wokeness, this movement is able to construct a coherence it otherwise lacks. Devoid of a clear vision of what it stands for, it is focused on opposition – like other right-wing movements before it.

The starting point of this mobilisation is, and has always been, race. The white supremacist 'Great Replacement Theory' posits that non-white populations are replacing whites through migration and demographic changes. Once a fringe conspiracy theory, it is now being openly espoused on *Fox News*.

Electoral laws are also being passed to disenfranchise Black voters, and bans are being placed on teaching the history of how southern states maintained white power through systems of racial disenfranchisement.

Trump and DeSantis are now fuelling and feeding off this agenda as they seek to build their political careers. But they can only do so because there is a large existing social constituency hungry for such actions, built on generations of opposition to progressive social gains.

The past is never dead. It's not even past.

Unpapering the cracks: Sugar, slavery and *The Sydney Morning Herald*

Sally Young
University of Melbourne

In a splash of articles in early 2023, the British *Guardian* acknowledged and apologised for its historical links with slavery. The Scott Trust, owners of the newspaper that became a global news website, outlined how *The Guardian*'s founders were linked to transatlantic slavery and announced a program of restorative justice. John Edward Taylor, the journalist who founded the *Manchester Guardian* in 1821, profited from partnerships with cotton manufacturers and merchants who imported raw cotton produced by enslaved people in Jamaica and in the Sea Islands along the coast of South Carolina and Georgia.

In Australia, our oldest surviving newspaper has its own historical links to the shameful practice of slave labour.

In 1841, John Fairfax (1804–77) became the first of five generations of Fairfax family owners of *The Sydney Morning Herald*, which had been founded in 1831 as *The Sydney Herald*. The Fairfax family also became major shareholders in Colonial Sugar Refining Company (CSR). CSR was founded in Sydney in 1855 by Edward Knox, but it descended from the Australasian Sugar Company, established in 1842. The precise date on which the Fairfax family became sugar investors is not known, but the family was certainly involved by 1855, when John Fairfax's daughter, Emily, married the general manager of CSR.

In the 1870s and 1880s, CSR expanded into milling cane in Queensland and Fiji. It profited from the use of what was effectively slave labour through the abduction and importation of tens of thousands of South Sea islanders, who were disparagingly called 'kanakas' (a Hawaiian word meaning 'man'). According to the Australian Human Rights Commission, between 1863 and 1904 'an estimated 55,000 to 62,500 Islanders were brought to Australia to labour on sugar-cane and cotton farms in Queensland and northern New South Wales'. They were forced to perform backbreaking labour in appalling conditions.

Most came from Vanuatu and the Solomon Islands, but they also arrived from more than seventy other Pacific islands. CSR chartered ships for the express purpose of 'recruiting' labourers from these islands.

Men, women and children, some as young as nine, were forced, coerced or tricked into coming to Australia. The practice of kidnapping them was known as 'blackbirding' ('blackbird' was another word for slave).

Although a system of indentured labour was later established, Pacific islanders were still exploited, denied basic rights and paid miserable wages. In 1901, two Acts of parliament facilitated their mass deportation as part of establishing the White Australia policy.

Although *The Sydney Morning Herald* was normally a strong supporter of the White Australia policy, the paper wanted it suspended in the case of the cane fields. In August 1901, it argued there was a special need for 'black' labour in the sugar fields of Queensland because the task was not suitable for white men:

> The sun, so deadly to the white man, is to [the 'kanaka'] only the source of a genial warmth … these islanders are [like] the Australian aborigine [sic] … just sufficiently intelligent for work in the canefield … cheap, and … inured to outdoor labour in a tropical climate.

A group of South Sea islander farm workers on a sugar plantation at Cairns in 1890 (State Library of Queensland)

The paper argued that 'white men' were still getting 'all the work calling for intelligence'. And, if the 'kanakas' had to go, then the sugar planter should be given some other form of help such as a duty on sugar. At no stage did the paper declare its owners' interest in the issue.

Like the mining giant Broken Hill Proprietary (BHP), CSR became a powerful monopoly in Australia. Both were helped along by friends in the press – newspaper owners who were heavily invested in companies they were promoting and demanding government assistance for. (The Fairfaxes were also shareholders in BHP, as were other newspaper families, including the Symes and the Baillieus.)

Although most Pacific island labourers had been deported from Australia by 1908, CSR continued to prosper off the back of indentured (mostly Indian) labourers in Fiji, where there were severe working conditions and high mortality rates. By 1910, CSR was one of the three largest companies in Australia.

In 1915, the federal government granted CSR protection via an embargo on imported sugar. In 1923, the Queensland Government signed an agreement with CSR that meant the company effectively had a monopoly on sugar production (which lasted until 1989).

By 1930, CSR was the wealthiest company in Australia and the Fairfaxes were among the country's wealthiest families. The family's links with CSR were still active in the 1960s. By then, CSR had branched out into industrial chemicals, building materials and, disastrously, asbestos.

The longstanding connection between CSR and the Fairfaxes was not widely known in the mid-20th century, nor would it have attracted much interest then, let alone condemnation on the basis of CSR's history of forced labour. On the contrary, in a newspaper industry filled with ruthless proprietors, including liars, thugs and crooks, the Fairfaxes had a reputation for being decent, moral and ethical. They were known for being cultured, civic-minded and philanthropic.

The Fairfaxes controlled *The Sydney Morning Herald* for 149 years, until 1990, when a misguided takeover action mounted by young Warwick Fairfax ended in financial disaster. Since 2019, *The Sydney Morning Herald* (along with *The Age* and *The Australian Financial Review*) has been owned by the Nine group, a television company founded by the Fairfaxes' nemesis, Frank Packer, a rival newspaper and magazine owner in Sydney.

Packer was not known for his philanthropy, nor for holding enlightened attitudes on racial equality.

Racism was often blatantly expressed in newspaper pages, encouraging oppression, discrimination and inhumane treatment, including in the sugar plantations of Queensland. In 1935, *The Sydney Morning Herald* conceded that blackbirding – a practice it had implicitly supported in the 1890s and early 1900s – was actually a 'type of slavery'.

Now would be a good time for Australia's oldest newspaper to follow the lead of *The Guardian* and investigate and acknowledge how its own growth in the 19th and 20th centuries was connected to that slavery.

Editor's note: Comment was sought from the editor of The Sydney Morning Herald *for this article but no reply had been provided at the time of writing.*

PART III

Coping with economic pressure

In 2023, we tried to hang on to the good economic times. It's about to get harder

Peter Martin
Economics Editor, The Conversation
Australian National University

As unlikely as it seems with all the talk about recession, Australia began 2023 in pretty good economic shape.

After Russia's invasion of Ukraine in early 2022, inflation exploded to levels that were the worst in a generation. But at the start of 2023, every one of the twenty-nine forecasters surveyed by The Conversation expected inflation to decrease from its peak of 7.8 per cent – as it did, in line with steady falls overseas.

And the jobs market was better than it had been in half a century. Australia's unemployment rate was moving between 3.4 per cent and 3.5 per cent – way below the 6–7 per cent typical of the past fifty years. It was the lowest unemployment rate since 'Billy, Don't Be a Hero' topped the music charts in 1974.

Before COVID, there typically had been three times as many unemployed people as vacant jobs. But after three years of border closures and stimulus spending, the ratio was close to one-to-one. Statistically, there was a job available for almost everyone who wanted one.

And part-time jobs were being converted into full-time jobs at an extraordinary rate. While total employment had climbed by 238,000 jobs during 2022, full-time employment had climbed by twice as much – 538,000. Hours worked grew at three times the rate of population growth, which was itself taking off after years of zero or negligible immigration during lockdowns.

And wage growth was finally starting to climb, too. After a decade in which it couldn't even reach 3 per cent, wage growth climbed to 3.4 per cent during 2022 and was heading up as inflation was set to head down.

Suddenly, Reserve Bank decisions mattered

So, what could go wrong? One thing was the cumulative impact of the eight consecutive increases in interest rates the Reserve Bank of Australia (RBA) had imposed between May and December 2022, lifting the best available mortgage rate from 2.6 per cent to more than 5 per cent at a time when the typical new mortgage exceeded $600,000.

Another was the series of further interest rate rises the RBA was about to unleash throughout 2023, enough to push up repayments on recent mortgages by a hard-to-bear $1000 a month – all because the bank wanted to be sure inflation was really coming down.

Those rate hikes were among the most consequential decisions anyone could have made. And they took place in an environment that was anything but perfect for measured decision-making.

The six-year term of RBA governor Philip Lowe was set to expire in September; Michele Bullock had been named his successor two months earlier. It's traditional for a governor to hand his successor an economy in good working order. That's what Lowe's predecessor did for him. However, Lowe was in the job for two years and nine months before he felt the need to adjust rates. This made ensuring inflation really was on the way down and headed back towards the RBA's 2–3 per cent target band more urgent than it otherwise might have been.

Treasurer Jim Chalmers commissioned and published a 280-page review of the way the RBA works – the first in its 64-year history. The review recommended the bank's 2–3 per cent inflation target be tightened to aim for the mid-point (2.5 per cent), 'in order to maximise the chance that the target is met and best anchor inflation expectations'.

The bank would be forced to explain how long inflation was 'expected to be materially away from the midpoint of the target and why', all of which added greater-than-usual urgency to the task of bringing down an inflation rate that was already falling.

Recession became a real possibility

With the May Budget forecasting economic growth of just 1.5 per cent in 2023–24 – the lowest in fifty years outside of a recession – the risk of cutting rates too far and too quickly and bringing on an actual recession became ever more present. Not that it would have made much practical difference to the lives of many Australians. Forecast economic growth of 1.5 per cent at a time when the population was growing by 2 per cent meant a per-capita recession. Consumer spending climbed in absolute terms through 2023, but when it was adjusted for price growth and population growth, it became apparent what was being bought per person was falling.

Other decisions mattered less than the RBA's. In June, the Fair Work Commission lifted the minimum wage broadly in line with inflation, as it always did. The Budget also recorded an unexpected surplus, due in part to unexpectedly high iron ore prices and to the strong employment growth the Coalition had bequeathed to Labor by spending big on programs such as JobKeeper in the early years of COVID.

Electricity and gas prices jumped in July despite efforts to hold them back. For most customers, the increase in regulated prices was 21–24 per cent. The government said if it hadn't intervened to cap wholesale gas and coal prices in late 2022, the increase would have been 40–50 per cent.

The government claimed its biggest economic challenge (presumably apart from avoiding a recession) was getting productivity growing again. Labour productivity had been falling since March 2022. But that's largely because of what labour productivity is: output per hour worked. Hours worked soared from 2022 well into 2023 as employment increased, and it was unreasonable to expect output to climb by as much at the same time.

Productivity and tax are about to matter

The government identified lifting productivity as the key means of raising living standards when it released its three-yearly *Intergenerational Report* in the second half of 2023. However, back in March, it had simply published a Productivity Commission report that presented it with seventy-one recommendations for lifting productivity, without responding – just as, five years earlier, the previous government had simply published a Productivity Commission report that presented it with twenty-eight recommendations for lifting productivity, without responding.

One decision the government won't be able to put off for much longer is whether to rework the gargantuan Stage 3 tax cuts legislated half a decade ago by then-treasurer Scott Morrison and due to finally come into force in mid-2024. Whether they turn out to be well timed by then is anyone's guess. But they are expensive ($313 billion over a decade) and give difficult-to-justify tax cuts of $9000 to high earners on $200,000, while giving just $875 to more-average earners on $80,000.

The decisions the government makes about tax in the years ahead will say a lot about how it plans to tackle Australia's two big emerging divides: between lightly taxed, well-off retirees and younger working Australians, and between Australians able to buy homes and those who fear they never will.

Taxing the capital gains on high-end family homes would be one way to do it. Winding back the ability to negatively gear properties (as Labor promised in the 2016 and 2019 election campaigns) would be another. As would taxing the superannuation earnings of retirees so they are treated the same as the super earnings of younger Australians. And including homes in the pension assets test.

Incrementalism might not cut it

It's true governments have become more cautious than they used to be – 2023 marked the fiftieth anniversary of prime minister Gough Whitlam's dramatic July 1973 decision to slash every single import tariff by 25 per cent at midnight – but it is also true that slow change might not be enough.

In 2023, former Treasury secretary Ken Henry reflected on the failure of the Rudd government's apparently bold response to his 2010 tax review, which he said actually amounted to just one measure – a mining superprofits tax. He said the lesson was: 'If you give a lot of well-armed people only one target to shoot, it will take a pounding.'

The best chance of success comes with making a raft of much-needed big changes, and to make them all at once. But such an assault requires time to prepare, and time to build the case. Prime Minister Anthony Albanese and Chalmers don't have much time: 2024 will be the year before the next election.

One way to make sure they and future governments can genuinely govern and do what's right would be to elect them for four-year rather than three-year terms. We could put the idea to the next referendum.

The housing wealth gap between older and younger Australians has widened alarmingly in the past thirty years. Here's why

Rachel Ong ViforJ
Curtin University
Christopher Phelps
Curtin University

The housing wealth gap between younger and older Australians is undeniably growing. Our study, published in January 2023, attempted to find out how much it has grown by estimating the gap in the home equity of older people (Australians in their fifties) and younger people (Australians in their thirties) in 1997–98 and 2017–18.

Our findings, adjusted for inflation, show that in 1997–98, the younger group had mean housing equity of $97,799 compared to the older group's $255,323. This meant the older group had 161 per cent more home equity than the younger group, or 2.6 times as much. By 2017–18, the younger group had mean equity of $140,080 but the older group's mean equity had increased more, to $467,182. The older group had 234 per cent more equity than the younger group, or 3.3 times as much.

The housing wealth gap between the old and young had grown from 161 per cent to 234 per cent, making it almost half as big again.

The increase in the gap between those we describe as the income-poor young and the income-rich old was even more alarming, a doubling from 532 per cent to 1230 per cent.

Two things have widened the divide

Our study draws on the 1997–98 and 2017–18 Australian Bureau of Statistics (ABS) surveys of income and housing and identifies two forces widening the gap.

The first relates to home ownership. While ownership rates for both groups have fallen, the decline has been steeper among the young (falling from 52 per cent to 40 per cent) than the old (80 per cent to 69 per cent).

The second relates to the different trajectories in the growth of home equity among those who do own homes. In 1997–98, the average equity in the primary home of owners in the older group was 1.7 times that of owners in the younger group. By 2017–18, it was twice that of the younger owners.

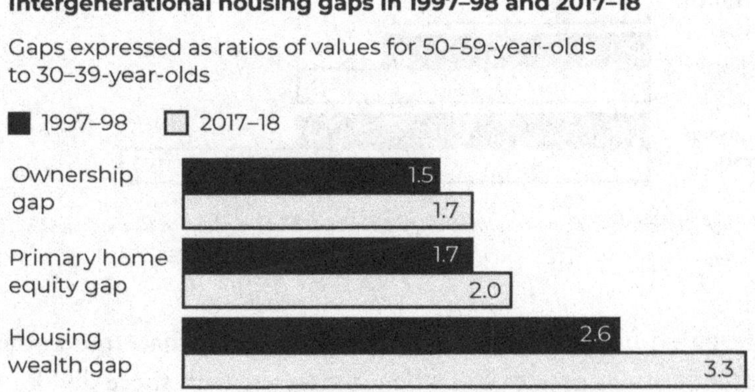

Source: Ong ViforJ and Phelps, 'The Growing Intergenerational Housing Wealth Divide', 2023. Created with Datawrapper.

The increasing ownership gap turns out to have mattered more than the increasing gap in equity among those who do have homes.

We found that if the ownership gap had not widened, the overall intergenerational housing wealth gap would have been smaller at 200 per cent, rather than 234 per cent. If the gap in home equity among those who owned homes had not widened, the gap would have been smaller at 215 per cent rather than 234 per cent.

It's not just age – there are other divides

Housing inequality exists across other divides. We identified gaps across gender, location and income divides:

- Comparing single women to single men, we find the advantage enjoyed by single women has shrunk from 72 per cent to 42 per cent.
- Comparing Australians in regional and urban areas, we find the advantage enjoyed by those in cities has climbed from 46 per cent to 93 per cent.
- Comparing Australians in the bottom and top thirds of income (adjusted for family size), we find the housing wealth gap has widened from 94 per cent to 191 per cent.

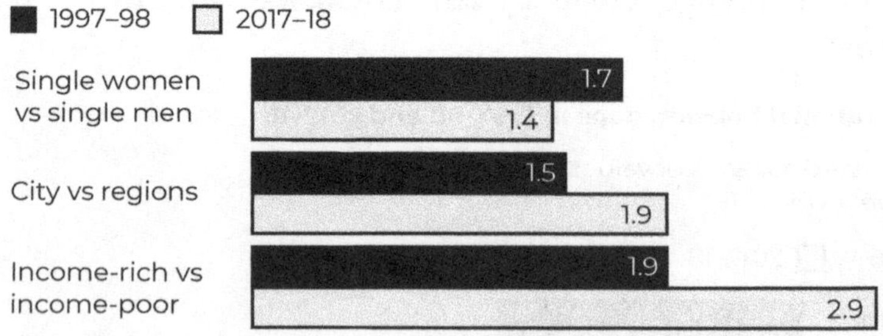

Source: Ong ViforJ and Phelps, 'The Growing Intergenerational Housing Wealth Divide', 2023. Created with Datawrapper.

The age-based housing wealth gap is much greater than these other divides, but it becomes greater still when it interacts with those divides.

The greatest combined divide is between people who are both younger and income-poor and people who are both older and income-rich. In 1997–98, the housing wealth gap between these two groups was an outsized 532 per cent. Over the following two decades, it more than doubled to 1230 per cent.

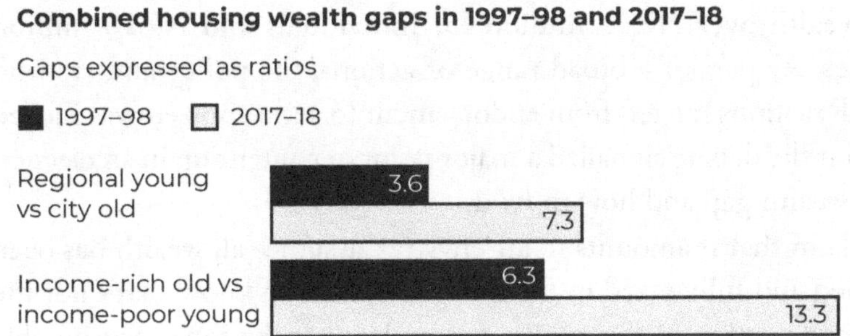

Source: Ong ViforJ and Phelps, 'The Growing Intergenerational Housing Wealth Divide', 2023. Created with Datawrapper.

The need for action is becoming urgent

Our findings put beyond doubt the claim that younger people are falling further behind older people in terms of home ownership. While some of this might reflect a shift in young people's investment preferences towards non-housing assets, we found young non-owners also have less non-property wealth than owners.

This means the need to act on both the affordability of housing and the security of tenure for renters is urgent.

Our finding that older Australians enjoy higher growth in home values than young Australians provides support for encouraging the use of equity-release ('reverse mortgage') schemes to unlock their housing wealth, relieving younger Australians of some of the tax burden of supporting them. Although obstacles remain, the benefits to both older Australians and less well-off younger taxpayers would be considerable.

In the past thirty years, the housing wealth gap between income-poor young Australians and income-rich older Australians has doubled to more than 1000 per cent. Our society will hold together better if we do what we can to wind it back.

New Zealand's housing market drives inequality. Why not just tax houses like any other income?

Susan St John
University of Auckland

New Zealand's Green Party made waves this year when it proposed to tax net wealth over NZ$2 million for individuals and NZ$4 million for couples. As part of a broad range of actions, the policy aims to 'end poverty'. Reactions ranged from endorsement to accusations it was fuelled by envy, but the debate signalled a major point of contention in an election year: the wealth gap and how to fix it.

The claim that it amounts to an 'envy tax' assumes all wealth has been fully earned and fully taxed in the first place. But we know that's not the case. A good portion of the wealth accumulated at the top is attributable to fortunate circumstances generating significant tax-free gains.

Inland Revenue's recent survey of the wealthiest 311 NZ families revealed an average net worth of NZ$276 million. At the same time, we know many households are struggling with the rising cost of living. According to Stats NZ, around 155,000 households feel their incomes aren't sufficient to meet everyday basic needs. Food banks report ever-rising numbers of families unable to feed themselves.

The major source of this lopsided wealth is the housing market. New Zealand has seen the biggest housing boom in the Western world. Property owners have ridden the wave to make large, tax-free capital gains, while others languish in substandard emergency housing or are forced to live in garages or cars.

Far too much of our scarce labour, building materials, imported fixtures and land have been diverted to unproductive high-end housing, leaving too little to meet the real housing need. Because it isn't taxed properly, investing in housing has been encouraged as a way to accumulate wealth.

The trouble with a wealth tax

While the Greens' wealth tax is a useful start to a wider discussion of inequality, it inevitably creates obstacles that in the end may be too difficult to overcome. Probably the biggest hurdle is that this kind of tax can be incredibly complex and would provoke endless debate about what should be included.

The Greens' proposal, for example, would capture business assets, shares, art above a certain value, and cars above NZ$50,000. But what if you have two cars worth NZ$49,000 each? Why should they be excluded when one valued at NZ$80,000 is included?

And how is debt factored into calculations of net wealth? House mortgages may be straightforward, but what about credit card debt, car finance or borrowing to finance overseas travel?

Not a capital gains tax

For all these reasons, it's time to stop debating notions of a confiscatory wealth tax and make the issue simply one of treating all income the same for tax purposes.

Instead of a complicated net wealth tax on everything, let's start with the biggest culprit – housing. This would address the under-taxation of income from holding housing as an asset. This is not the same as a capital gains tax – those days are over. Numerous tax working groups have failed over thirty years to make headway on this. Politically, it is a dead duck.

Besides, the real problems – inequality and misallocation of resources – wouldn't be touched by a capital gains tax. Such a tax can only apply to gains made on houses sold in the future, not the accumulated gains over many years, and it will always exempt the family home.

How a house tax works

Instead, let's take the total value of all housing held by each individual, subtract registered first mortgages, and allow a NZ$1 million exemption to reflect that everyone is entitled to a basic family home. Then we treat this net equity as if it was in a term deposit generating a taxable interest return. When houses are held in trusts and companies, in most cases the income will be taxed at the trust or company rate with no exemption.

Calculated annually and pegged to the capital value of properties, this effective income would be taxed at the person's marginal tax rate. It would affect those with second homes, multiple rentals or high-value properties, but it would not significantly affect the great majority of home owners, who have much less than NZ$1 million of net equity. Thus, a couple living in a NZ$3 million house with a NZ$1 million mortgage would fall under the threshold.

This approach would help put investment in housing, after a basic home, on the same footing as money in the bank or in shares. Better choices for the use of scarce housing resources should follow.

Landlords would no longer need expensive accountants to minimise taxable rental income. And it would reduce the blight of 'ghost houses' and residential land banking.

A circuit breaker

The simplicity of this income approach means the government can build on the existing tax system. It lives up to the mantra of a 'broad base, low rate' tax system and affects only the very wealthy and those whose tax rates are highest. Moreover, it could be implemented quickly, using existing property valuations and registered mortgages, unlike a net wealth tax where the devil is in the contentious detail.

The effect should be positive for those struggling in the housing market, as more housing for sale or rent is opened up. Good landlords should welcome the greater simplicity. In the longer term, the extra taxable income could produce revenue for redistribution and social investment. Critically, it would start to give the right price signals to reduce over-investment in luxury housing and real estate held for capital gain.

This approach is essentially a circuit breaker that can simply and quickly address the accumulation of wealth by a small group of people. Crucially, it has a sound economic rationale. By taking the first step and including luxury and investment housing returns that currently fly under the radar, it reduces the advantages of holding housing rather than more productive investments.

Tired of shrinking pay? The real drain on Australians' productivity is falling wages

Mark Humphery-Jenner
UNSW Sydney

When was the last time you got a pay increase? Was it anywhere near the rate of inflation? If it feels as if your wage is shrinking and cost-of-living pressures are growing, you're in good company. And it might just be harming productivity. Here's why.

Labor productivity – measured as gross domestic product (GDP) per hour worked – has been shrinking for a year now, after decades of reasonable, albeit declining, productivity growth throughout the 1980s, 1990s and the first two decades of the 2000s.

Source: ABS National Accounts, Table 1. Created with Datawrapper.

All sorts of reasons have been suggested. One is working from home. Commonwealth Bank CEO Matt Comyn has ordered staff to return to the office, saying there are 'certain types of work that are done more effectively in person'.

RBA research says it might be a resurgence in the proportion of wages set by industry awards rather than workplace agreements, meaning there's less scope for rewarding performance.

Another reason is weak wage growth itself.

Shrinking real wages are demotivating

We must also look at wages. Wages are falling in inflation-adjusted ('real') terms.

Adjusted for inflation, Australians are being paid less than they were in 2020.

The nominal versus the real average weekly wage

Real average weekly wage expressed in 1994 dollars

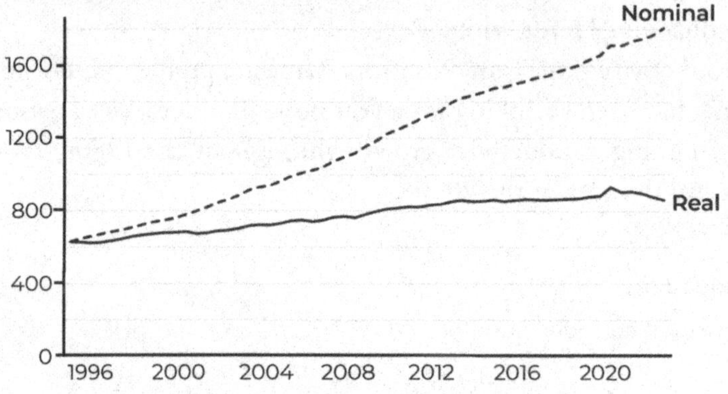

Average full-time adult ordinary time earnings

Source: ABS Average Weekly Earnings, Consumer Price Index. Created with Datawrapper.

Shrinking real wages are demotivating. While this is hardly a new insight, a bemusing number of people seem shocked by the idea that someone might be less keen to work when the real value of what they are paid is falling. Research on executive compensation established this as long ago as the 1970s.

The whole field of compensation contract theory is based on the insight that a person's sense of wellbeing goes up with money but down with perceived effort and risk. Money can induce people to work in ways they otherwise would not.

Company boards have long used incentives to encourage otherwise-cautious executives to take risks. They even tailor compensation contracts to executives' behavioural traits.

How do workers produce less?

Consciously or otherwise, workers whose real wages are falling might care less about their jobs. They might work more slowly, or produce worse-quality goods or services. And their attitude might migrate to other workers and to clients, undermining productivity more broadly. If this happens at enough corporations – and real wages are certainly falling at enough corporations – it will harm GDP per hour worked throughout the entire economy.

Sluggish wage growth can also affect the number of observed hours worked. When wage growth and incentives are strong, ambitious workers will work more than their contracted hours, and won't claim for it. They might work on the weekend and at night, easing staff scheduling and time-zone issues, helping the firm do what it needs to do.

Uncounted extra hours don't increase the 'hours' in GDP per hour, but they do increase the GDP, increasing measured productivity.

When people stop doing unpaid overtime, while their recorded hours might not much change, the GDP they produce declines. And there are reasons to believe that Australian workers are no longer going above and beyond to produce more to the extent they used to.

One is an increase in the number of Australians holding multiple jobs. Over the past five years, the proportion of Australian workers holding more than one job has climbed from 6 per cent to 6.7 per cent, which appears to be an all-time high.

Proportion of Australian workers holding multiple jobs

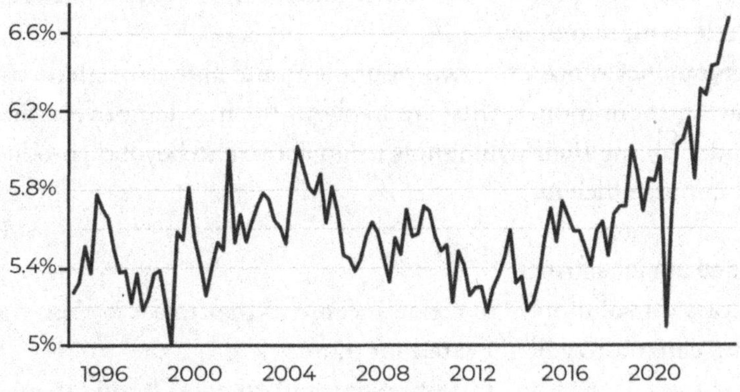

Seasonally adjusted, all industries

Source: ABS Labour Account. Created with Datawrapper.

These official figures understate the extent to which Australians are turning their focus away from their main jobs for three reasons:

- they exclude side hustles not counted as 'jobs'
- they exclude jobs in the cash economy
- they exclude workers whose 'new' second job is spending time with their family rather than working overtime.

The rise in multiple job holders is likely to both increase the total number of hours worked and reduce the effort workers put into their main jobs. And, as these second jobs are often more junior, it can result in highly skilled workers producing less per hour than they would have had they put the hours in their main job.

The overall picture is one of a demotivated workforce realising there is no longer much point in 'going the extra mile', 'going above and beyond', or buying into whatever the latest euphemism is.

Returning to the office might make things worse

Although returning to the office is touted as a way to boost productivity by building collaboration, it might well do the reverse. There is ample evidence to show that workers hate commuting. In capital cities, commuting can consume two hours per day in driving, parking and allowing time for unexpected delays.

It is also costly. Workers will tolerate it if there is no other choice or it is a clear path to more money.

But if companies reinstate a two-hour commute and associated costs without paying more money, they are likely to further demotivate their workers, undermining their willingness to 'go above and beyond', produce more and be more efficient.

What's needed are incentives

A straightforward solution is to create incentives that make it clear that workers who care more will get cared for more.

The incentives need to be in addition to standard raises. Using them as a cynical ploy to hold wages constant unless employees work ever harder will backfire.

The incentives must also be credible. It isn't enough to create the vague possibility of a promotion. Employers have to demonstrate that if their workers produce more, they will be paid more. And the extra pay needs to be enough to matter.

An even better solution would be job-hopping (switching jobs to get better rewards).

Australians have long been lethargic about changing jobs, allowing themselves to be hit with a 'loyalty tax' for staying put. An ABS survey for the year to February 2022 showed an overdue uptick in the proportion of workers switching jobs, from 7.5 per cent to 9.5 per cent; this remained at the same level for the year to February 2023.

An uptick in job-hopping

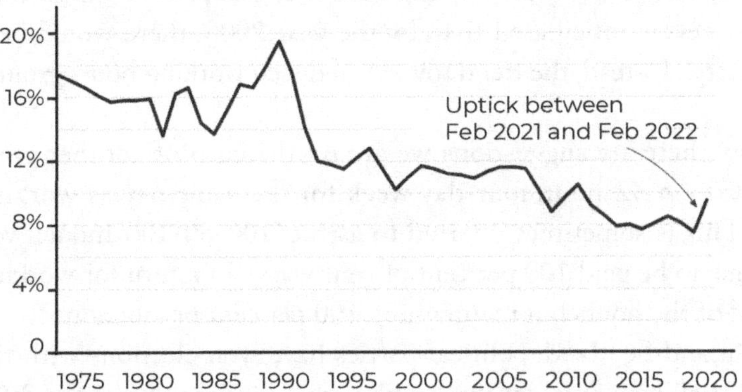

Source: ABS Job Mobility Survey. Created with Datawrapper.

The importance of job-hopping as a means of incentivising both workers and employers makes Labor's proposed expansion of industry-wide enterprise bargaining a bad idea. If employers set wages together, they are unlikely to set them differently.

In any event, there is little sign that employers are interested in motivating their workers to produce more. It's easier to blame workers and make a case for small pay rises.

Four-day work week trials have been labelled a 'resounding success', but four big questions need answers

Anthony Veal
University of Technology Sydney

A little more than a century ago, most people in industrialised countries worked sixty hours a week – six ten-hour days. A forty-hour work week of five eight-hour days became the norm, along with more paid holidays, in the 1950s. These changes were made possible by massive increases in productivity and hard-fought struggles by workers with bosses for a fair share of the expanding economic pie.

In the 1960s and 1970s, it was expected that this pattern would continue. It was even anticipated that, by the year 2000, there would be a 'leisure society'. Instead, the trend towards reduced working hours ground to a halt.

But now there are suggestions we are on the cusp of another great leap forward – a 32-hour, four-day week for the same pay as working five days. This is sometimes referred to as the '100-80-100' model: you will continue to be paid 100 per cent of your wages in return for working 80 per cent of the hours but maintaining 100 per cent production.

In Spain and Scotland, political parties have won elections with the promise of trialling a four-day week, although a similar move in the 2019 UK general election was unsuccessful. In Australia, a Senate committee inquiry has recommended a national trial of the four-day week.

Hopes of the four-day week becoming reality have been buoyed by glowing reports about the success of trials in which employers have reported cutting hours but maintaining productivity. However, impressive as these trial results may appear, it's still not clear whether the model would work across the economy.

An employer-led movement

Unlike previous campaigns for a shorter work week, the four-day work week movement is being led by employers in a few, mainly English-speaking, countries. Notable is Andrew Barnes, owner of a NZ financial services company, who founded the 4 Day Week Global organisation. It has coordinated a program of four-day work week trials in six countries: Australia, Canada, Ireland, New Zealand, the United Kingdom and the

United States. Almost 100 companies and more than 3000 employees have been involved. (A highly publicised trial in Iceland was not coordinated by this organisation.)

These trials are being monitored by an 'international collaboration' of research teams at three universities: Boston College, Cambridge University and University College Dublin. The Boston College team is led by work-time/leisure-time guru Juliet Schor, author of the 1991 bestseller *The Overworked American*.

A number of reports have been published, including one 'global' report covering all six countries, and separate reports for the United Kingdom and Ireland. A report on the Australian and New Zealand trials, involving twenty-six companies and 758 employees, was published in May 2023. Overall, these reports have declared the trials a 'resounding success', both for employers and employees.

Employees, unsurprisingly, were overwhelmingly positive. They reported less stress, burnout, fatigue and work–family conflict, and better physical and mental health. More significant were the employers' responses. They generally reported improved employee morale and no loss of revenue. Nearly all have committed to, or are considering, continuing with the four-day work week model.

Four big questions

However, the trials do not answer all the questions about the viability of the four-day work week. The four main ones are as follows.

First, are the research results reliable? Employers and employees were surveyed at the start, halfway through and at the end of the six-month trials. But only about half of the employees and two-thirds of employers completed the vital final round. So, there's some uncertainty about their representativeness.

Second, did the participating firms demonstrate the key productivity proposition: an increase of almost 20 per cent in output per employee per hour worked? The firms involved were not asked to provide 'output' data, just revenue. This may be a reasonable substitute, but it may also have been affected by price movements (inflation was on the march in 2022).

Third, for those firms that achieved the claimed productivity increase, how did it come about? And is it sustainable? Proponents of the four-day work week argue that employees are more productive because they work in a more concentrated way, ignoring distractions. A much longer period than six months will be needed to establish whether this more intense work pattern is sustainable.

Finally, is the four-day model likely to be applicable across the whole economy? This is the key question, the answer to which will only emerge over time. The organisations involved in the trials were self-selected and unrepresentative of the economy as a whole. They employed mostly office-based workers. Almost four-fifths were in managerial, professional, information technology and clerical occupations. Organisations in other sectors, with different occupational profiles, may find increased productivity through more intensive working difficult to emulate.

Take manufacturing. Only three firms from this sector were included in the large UK trial. Since manufacturing has been subject to efficiency studies and labour-saving investment for a century or more, an overall 20 per cent 'efficiency gain' to be had across the board seems unlikely.

Then there are sectors that provide face-to-face services to the public, often seven days a week. They cannot close for a day, and their work intensity is often governed by health and safety concerns. Reduced hours are unlikely to be covered by individual productivity increases. To maintain operating hours, either staff will have to work overtime or more staff would need to be employed.

As for the public sector, in Australia and other countries, 'efficiency savings' involving budget cuts of about 2 per cent a year have been common for decades. Any 'slack' is likely to have been already squeezed out of the system. Again, reducing standard hours would result in the need to pay overtime rates or recruit extra staff, at extra cost.

So what now?

This does not mean the four-day work week could not spread through the economy. One scenario is that it could spread in those workplaces and sectors where productivity gains are achievable. Those employers and sectors not offering reduced hours would find it harder to recruit staff. They would need to reduce hours, perhaps by stages, to compete. In the absence of productivity gains, they would be forced to absorb the extra costs or pass them on in increased prices.

The pace at which such change takes place will depend, as it always has, on the level of economic growth, productivity trends and labour market conditions. But it is unlikely to happen overnight. And, as always, it will be accompanied by many employers and their representatives claiming the sky is about to fall in.

If you haven't joined a union, it's time you paid to benefit from union deals

Jim Stanford
University of Sydney

A long-overdue public debate has begun in Australia about 'free riding' in industrial relations. This is when non-union members benefit from collective agreements negotiated by union members without contributing (through membership dues or other payments) to their negotiation and administration.

Several union leaders want rules to stop free riding. Without this, they argue, union membership will keep falling, imperilling collective bargaining. The issue has been given impetus by the latest data on union membership rates. The proportion of employees belonging to a union is now at a record low of 12.5 per cent. In the private sector, it's just 8 per cent.

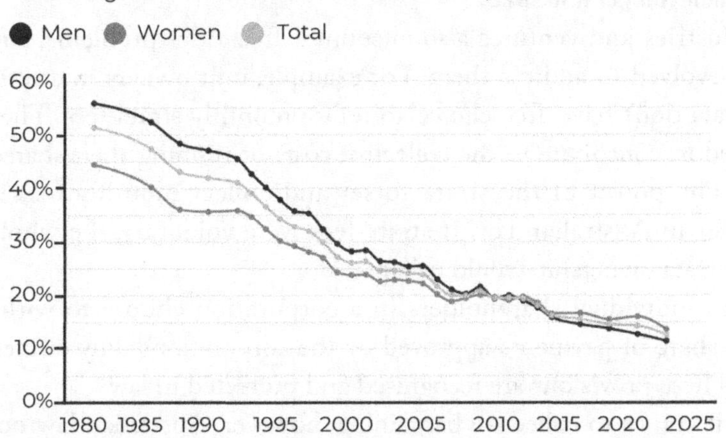

Source: ABS. Made with Flourish.

In the 1980s, more than half of the Australian workforce was unionised. Since then, Australia has experienced the most dramatic de-unionisation of any major industrial country. That, at least in part, is by design. The Howard government passed laws in the late 1990s and 2000s prohibiting union preferences in hiring, bargaining fees or other structured supports for union membership.

But the idea that workers can get something for nothing – enjoying the benefits of collective bargaining without contributing to its costs – ignores both economic theory and reality.

The economics of free riding

Economists have long grappled with the problem of free riders in many areas of economic life. The textbook case involves 'public goods' – things to which access cannot be limited to paying customers. Examples are clean air and water, infrastructure, policing and national defence.

With public goods, conventional market mechanisms (based on 'rational' individual choice) do not work. If something is 'free to all', there will be some people prepared to voluntarily contribute to its cost, and others who won't.

To address this market failure, economists endorse policy interventions that deliberately interfere with individual 'choice'. For government-provided public goods, this usually relies on compulsory contributions (taxes).

Why pay when you get it for free?

Other industries and ventures also encounter free-rider problems, and laws have evolved to address them. For example, unit owners in a residential strata don't have 'free choice' to refuse monthly strata fees. They are required to contribute to the collective costs of running their shared building. The power of the strata to set and collect monthly fees is provided for in Australian law. If strata fees were voluntary, the whole system of strata ownership would collapse.

Nor can individual shareholders in a corporation choose to withhold their share of payments approved by the corporation's duly elected directors. These provisions are recognised and protected in law.

When it comes to collective bargaining, however, Australian law not only tolerates but effectively encourages free riding. Under the *Fair Work*

Act, any benefit or entitlement (from higher wages to working conditions to rostering systems) negotiated through enterprise bargaining must be equally available to all workers covered by an agreement.

A narrowly 'rational' individual might understandably ask why they should join the union when they can get all the benefits of a union-negotiated contract anyway. Left to individual 'choice' in this context, it's not surprising union membership has fallen.

How other nations deal with the problem

I have catalogued six distinct approaches taken by other nations to address this market failure and establish a viable foundation for collective bargaining. All are founded on the presumption that collective bargaining is socially beneficial and should be encouraged.

One approach, informed by traditional conceptions of property rights, is to 'close off' access to union-negotiated wages and benefits to dues-paying members only. Varieties of this strategy have been tried in the United States and in New Zealand. This has generally not worked, however, because employers can still undermine unions by voluntarily offering equal improvements to non-members. It also damages worker solidarity, critical to any collective organisation.

Britain, Canada, India and Japan (among others) allow 'closed shop' or 'agency shop' arrangements. In any workplace that has been unionised (through some kind of majority decision, like a ballot or petition), all covered workers pay dues to reflect the benefits they receive from the collective agreement. In a closed shop, they must join the union; in an agency shop, they don't have to join the union but do have to pay the same fees.

The Philippines, South Africa and the United States are among those countries with a modified agency shop system called 'bargaining fees'. Everyone covered by an enterprise agreement, which must be ratified by the affected workers, contributes something (usually less than full union dues) to the direct costs of negotiating and administering that agreement.

France and Brazil are among several countries that directly support collective negotiations with public subsidies. Like paying taxes for public goods, this approach directly allocates resources to fund a service (collective bargaining) deemed to be essential for a healthy labour market. New Zealand is taking a similar approach with its Fair Pay Agreements (in effect since December 2022).

In Germany, Italy and many other European countries, collective bargaining is mandated by law, with employers above a certain size required to establish a workers council and cover the costs. Workers don't have to join the union but, with such well-funded infrastructure, collective bargaining remains strong.

In the Nordic countries and Belgium, extra support for collective bargaining is provided through union sponsorship of income support and social programs (like unemployment insurance and pensions). Workers are enticed to join their union to get better access to these services. This provides unions with resources and leverage for collective bargaining.

Developing an Australian-made fix

So, there is a wide choice of specific ways to fix the free-rider problem in industrial relations. In Australia, however, the right to free ride is fully protected, even celebrated. The result (as intended) has been the steady erosion of union membership. Australia is now quickly converging with the United States as one of the least unionised nations in the Organisation for Economic Cooperation and Development (OECD).

In December 2022, the Albanese government passed its Secure Jobs, Better Pay Bill, aimed at strengthening collective bargaining. If these reforms succeed in broadening collective bargaining coverage, the evidence suggests Australia's abysmal wage growth will pick up. That alone should enhance workers' appreciation of the value of collective action, and indirectly strengthen the incentive for union membership.

Eventually, however, it will need to be recognised that collective bargaining is not free, and is being undermined by a legal framework that pretends it is. We need to develop a made-in-Australia solution to fix it.

PART IV

A new era of exploration

AI pioneer Geoffrey Hinton says AI is a new form of intelligence unlike our own. Have we been getting it wrong this whole time?

Olivier Salvado
Lead AI for Missions, CSIRO
Jon Whittle
Director of Data61, CSIRO

Debates about artificial intelligence often characterise it as a technology that has come to compete with human intelligence. Indeed, one of the most widely pronounced fears is that AI may achieve human-like intelligence and render humans obsolete in the process.

However, one of the world's top AI scientists is now describing AI as a new form of intelligence – one that poses unique risks and will therefore require unique solutions. Geoffrey Hinton stepped down from his role at Google this year to warn the world about the dangers of AI. He follows in the steps of more than 1000 technology leaders who signed an open letter calling for a global halt to the development of advanced AI for at least six months.

Hinton's argument is nuanced. While he does think AI has the capacity to become smarter than humans, he also proposes it should be thought of as an altogether different form of intelligence to our own.

Why Hinton's ideas matter

Although experts have been raising red flags for some time, Hinton's decision to voice his concerns was significant.

Dubbed the 'godfather of AI', he has helped pioneer many of the methods underlying the modern AI systems we see today. His early work on neural networks led to him being one of three individuals awarded the 2018 Turing Award. And one of his students, Ilya Sutskever, went on to become a co-founder of OpenAI, the organisation behind ChatGPT.

When Hinton speaks, the AI world listens. And if we're to seriously consider his framing of AI as an intelligent, non-human entity, one could argue we've been thinking about it all wrong.

The false equivalence trap

On one hand, large, language model–based tools such as ChatGPT produce text that's very similar to what humans write. ChatGPT even makes stuff up, or 'hallucinates', which Hinton points out is something humans do as well. But we risk being reductive when we consider such similarities a basis for comparing AI intelligence with human intelligence.

We can find a useful analogy in the invention of artificial flight. For thousands of years, humans tried to fly by imitating birds: flapping their arms with some contraption mimicking feathers. This didn't work. Eventually, we realised fixed wings create uplift, using a different principle, and this heralded the invention of flight.

Planes are no better or worse than birds; they are different. They do different things and face different risks.

AI (and computation, for that matter) is a similar story. Large language models such as GPT-3 are comparable to human intelligence in many ways, but they work differently. ChatGPT crunches vast swathes of text to predict the next word in a sentence. Humans take a different approach to forming sentences. Both are impressive.

How is AI intelligence unique?

Both AI experts and non-experts have long drawn a link between AI and human intelligence, not to mention the tendency to anthropomorphise AI. But AI is fundamentally different to us in several ways. As Hinton explains:

> If you or I learn something and want to transfer that knowledge to someone else, we can't just send them a copy … But I can have 10,000 neural networks, each having their own experiences, and any of them can share what they learn instantly. That's a huge difference. It's as if there were 10,000 of us, and as soon as one person learns something, all of us know it.

AI outperforms humans on many tasks, including any task that relies on assembling patterns and information gleaned from large datasets. Humans are sluggishly slow in comparison and have less than a fraction of AI's memory.

Yet humans have the upper hand on some fronts. We make up for our poor memory and slow processing speed by using common sense and logic. We can quickly and easily learn how the world works, and use this knowledge to predict the likelihood of events. AI still struggles with this (although researchers are working on it).

Humans are also very energy-efficient, whereas AI requires powerful computers (especially for learning) that use orders of magnitude more energy than us. As Hinton puts it, 'humans can imagine the future … on a cup of coffee and a slice of toast'.

Okay, so what if AI is different to us?

If AI is fundamentally a different intelligence to ours, then it follows that we can't (or shouldn't) compare it to ourselves. A new intelligence presents new dangers to society and will require a paradigm shift in the way we talk about and manage AI systems. In particular, we may need to reassess the way we think about guarding against the risks of AI.

One of the basic questions that has dominated these debates is how to define AI. After all, AI is not binary. Intelligence exists on a spectrum, and the spectrum for human intelligence may be very different from that for machine intelligence. This very point was the downfall of one of the earliest attempts to regulate AI back in 2017 in New York, when auditors couldn't agree on which systems should be classified as AI. Defining AI when designing regulation is challenging.

So, perhaps we should focus less on defining AI in a binary fashion and more on the specific consequences of AI-driven actions.

What risks are we facing?

The speed of AI uptake in industry has taken everyone by surprise, and some experts are worried about the future of work. IBM CEO Arvind Krishna has said his company could be replacing some 7800 back-office jobs with AI in the next five years. We'll need to adapt how we manage AI as it becomes increasingly deployed for tasks once completed by humans.

More worryingly, AI's ability to generate fake text, images and video is leading us into a new age of information manipulation. Our current methods of dealing with human-generated misinformation won't be enough to address it.

Hinton is also worried about the dangers of AI-driven autonomous weapons, and how bad actors may leverage them to commit all forms of atrocity.

These are just some examples of how AI – and specifically, different characteristics of AI – can bring risk to the human world. To regulate AI productively and proactively, we need to consider these specific characteristics, and not apply recipes designed for human intelligence.

The good news is humans have learned to manage potentially harmful technologies before, and AI is no different.

No, AI probably won't kill us all – and there's more to this fear campaign than meets the eye

Michael Timothy Bennett
Australian National University

Doomsaying is an old occupation. Artificial intelligence is a complex subject. It's easy to fear what you don't understand. These three truths go some way towards explaining the oversimplification and dramatisation plaguing discussions about AI.

This year, the non-profit Center for AI Safety published an open letter claiming that AI poses an existential threat to humankind. It was signed by industry figureheads, including Geoffrey Hinton and the chief executives of Google DeepMind, Open AI and Anthropic. However, I'd argue a healthy dose of scepticism is warranted when considering the AI doomsayer narrative. Upon close inspection, we see there are commercial incentives to manufacture fear in the AI space.

And as a researcher of artificial general intelligence (AGI), it seems to me the framing of AI as an existential threat has more in common with 17th-century philosophy than computer science.

Was ChatGPT a breakthrough?

When ChatGPT was released late in 2022, people were delighted, entertained and horrified. But ChatGPT isn't a research breakthrough as much as it is a product. The technology it's based on is several years old. An early version of its underlying model, GPT-3, was released in 2020 with many of the same capabilities. It just wasn't easily accessible online for everyone to play with.

Back in 2020 and 2021, I and many others wrote papers discussing the capabilities and shortcomings of GPT-3 and similar models – and the world carried on as always. Forward to today, and ChatGPT has had an incredible impact on society. What changed?

In March, Microsoft researchers published a paper claiming GPT-4 showed 'sparks of artificial general intelligence'. AGI is the subject of a variety of competing definitions, but for the sake of simplicity it can be understood as AI with human-level intelligence. Some immediately interpreted the Microsoft research as saying GPT-4 is an AGI. By the definitions of AGI I'm familiar with, this is certainly not true. Nonetheless, it added to the hype and furore, and it was hard not to get caught up in the panic. Scientists are no more immune to groupthink than anyone else.

The same day that paper was submitted, The Future of Life Institute published an open letter calling for a six-month pause on training AI models more powerful than GPT-4, to allow everyone to take stock and plan ahead. Some of the AI luminaries who signed it expressed concern that AGI poses an existential threat to humans, and that ChatGPT is too close to AGI for comfort.

Soon after, prominent AI safety researcher Eliezer Yudkowsky – who has been commenting on the dangers of superintelligent AI since well before 2020 – took things a step further. He claimed we were on a path to building a 'superhumanly smart AI', in which case 'the obvious thing that would happen' is 'literally everyone on Earth will die'. He even suggested that countries need to be willing to risk nuclear war to enforce compliance with AI regulation across borders.

I don't consider AI an imminent existential threat

One aspect of AI safety research is to address potential dangers AGI might present. It's a difficult topic to study because there is little agreement on what intelligence is and how it functions, let alone what a superintelligence might entail. As such, researchers must rely as much on speculation and philosophical argument as evidence and mathematical proof.

There are two reasons I'm not concerned by ChatGPT and its by-products.

First, it isn't even close to the sort of artificial superintelligence that might conceivably pose a threat to humankind. The models underpinning it are slow learners that require immense volumes of data to construct anything akin to the versatile concepts humans can concoct from only a few examples. In this sense, it's not 'intelligent'.

Second, many of the more catastrophic AGI scenarios depend on premises I find implausible. For instance, there seems to be a prevailing (but unspoken) assumption that sufficient intelligence amounts to limitless real-world power. If this were true, more scientists would be billionaires.

Cognition, as we understand it in humans, takes place as part of a physical environment (which includes our bodies), and this environment imposes limitations. The concept of AI as a 'software mind' unconstrained by hardware has more in common with 17th-century dualism (the idea that the mind and body are separable) than with contemporary theories of the mind existing as part of the physical world.

Why the sudden concern?

Still, doomsaying is old hat, and the events of the last few years probably haven't helped. But there may be more to this story than meets the eye. Among the prominent figures calling for AI regulation, many work for or have ties to incumbent AI companies. This technology is useful, and there is money and power at stake – so fear-mongering presents an opportunity.

Almost everything involved in building ChatGPT has been published in research anyone can access. OpenAI's competitors can (and have) replicated the process, and it won't be long before free and open-source alternatives flood the market. This point was made clearly in a memo purportedly leaked from Google entitled 'We have no moat, and neither does OpenAI'. A 'moat' is jargon for a way to secure your business against competitors.

Yann LeCun, who leads AI research at Meta, says these models should be open since they will become public infrastructure. He and many others are unconvinced by the AGI doom narrative.

Notably, Meta wasn't invited when US President Joe Biden met with the leadership of Google DeepMind and OpenAI this year. That's despite the fact that Meta is almost certainly a leader in AI research – it produced PyTorch, the machine-learning framework OpenAI used to make GPT-3.

At the White House meetings, OpenAI CEO Sam Altman suggested the US Government should issue licences to those who are trusted to responsibly train AI models. Licences, as Stability AI CEO Emad Mostaque puts it, 'are a kinda moat'.

Companies such as Google, OpenAI and Microsoft have everything to lose by allowing small, independent competitors to flourish. Bringing in licensing and regulation would help cement their position as market leaders, and hamstring competition before it can emerge. While regulation is appropriate in some circumstances, regulations that are rushed through will favour incumbents and suffocate small, free and open-source competition.

The rich are pouring millions into life-extension research, but does it have any ethical value?

Julian Koplin
Monash University

Christopher Gyngell
University of Melbourne

Sam Altman, the CEO of OpenAI, has invested US$180 million in Retro Biosciences, a company seeking to extend human life spans by ten healthy years. One way it plans to achieve this is by 'rejuvenating' blood. This idea is based on studies that found old mice showed signs of reversed ageing when given the blood of young mice.

Altman isn't the only Silicon Valley entrepreneur supporting life-extension efforts. PayPal co-founder Peter Thiel, Amazon founder Jeff Bezos and Google co-founder Larry Page have poured millions into projects that could profoundly affect how we live our lives.

The first question raised is scientific: could these technologies work? On this front, the jury is still out, and there are grounds for both optimism and scepticism.

The second question is just as important: even if life-span extension is feasible, would it be ethical?

We explain why some common ethical arguments against life-span extension aren't as solid as they might seem. And we put forth another, somewhat overlooked explanation for why trying to live forever might not be worth it.

Is it worth it if you still die anyway?

One might argue life-span extension merely pushes back the inevitable: that we will die. Any life saved will only be saved temporarily.

A life-span extension of ten years is akin to saving a drowning swimmer only for them to die in a traffic accident ten years later. Although we might be sad about their eventual death, we'd still be glad we saved them. The same is true of conventional medicine. If a doctor cures my pneumonia, I will eventually die of something else, but that doesn't mean the doctor or I will regret my being saved.

It's also worth taking a longer view of where life-span extension research could lead us. In the most optimistic scenarios put forth by experts, even modest short-term gains could help people add centuries to their lives, since the benefits of each intervention could cascade. For example, each extra year of life would increase the likelihood of surviving until the next big breakthrough.

Is it worth it if immortality could get boring?

Many have argued against life-span extension on ethical grounds, saying they wouldn't use these technologies. Why might somebody be opposed?

One worry is that a very long life might be undesirable. Philosopher Bernard Williams said life is made valuable through the satisfaction of what he calls 'categorical desires': desires that give us reasons to want to live. Williams expects these desires relate to major life projects, such as raising a child or writing a novel. He worries that, given a long enough life, we will run out of such projects. If so, immortality would become tedious.

It's unclear whether Williams is right. Some philosophers point out human memories are fallible, and certain desires could resurface as we forget earlier experiences. Others emphasise that our categorical desires evolve as our life experiences reshape our interests, and they might continue to do so over the course of a very long life.

In either case, our categorical desires, and hence our reasons for living, would not be exhausted over a very long life. Even if immortality did get tedious, this wouldn't count against modest life-span extensions. Many would argue eighty-something years isn't enough time to explore one's potential. Personally, we'd welcome another twenty or even fifty years to write a novel, or start a career as a DJ.

Is it worth it if poor people miss out?

Another worry regarding life-span extension technologies is egalitarian. These technologies will be expensive. It seems unjust for Silicon Valley billionaires to celebrate their 150th birthdays while the rest of us mostly die in our seventies and eighties.

This objection seems convincing. Most people welcome interventions that promote health equality, which is reflected in broader societal demands for universal health care. But there's an important nuance to think about here. Consider that universal healthcare systems promote equality by improving the situation of those who aren't well off. On the other hand, preventing the development of life-span extension technologies will worsen the situation of those who are well off.

The ethical desirability of equality based on 'levelling down' is unclear. The poorest Australians are twice as likely to die before age seventy-five than the richest. Yet few people would argue we should stop developing technologies to improve the health of those aged over seventy-five. Moreover, the price of life-span extension technologies would likely eventually come down.

The real problem

We think there's one serious ethical objection that applies to extreme cases of life extension. If humans routinely lived very long lives, this could reduce how adaptable our populations are and lead to social stagnation. Even modest increases in life expectancy would radically increase population size. To avoid overpopulation, we'd need to reduce birth rates, which would drastically slow generational turnover.

As one of us (Chris) has explored in previous research, this could be incredibly harmful to societal progress, because it may:

- increase our vulnerability to extinction threats
- jeopardise individual wellbeing
- impede moral advancement.

Many fields benefit from a regular influx of young minds coming in and building on the work of predecessors. Even if the brains of older scientists remained sharp, their 'confirmation bias' – a tendency to seek and interpret information in ways that confirm one's prior beliefs – could slow the uptake of new scientific theories.

Moral beliefs are also prone to confirmation bias. In a world of extended life spans, individuals whose moral views were set in their youth (perhaps more than 100 years ago) will remain in positions of power.

It seems likely our society's moral code is badly mistaken in at least some respects. After all, we think past societies were catastrophically mistaken in theirs, such as when they endorsed slavery, or rendered homosexuality illegal. Slowing generational turnover could delay the point at which we recognise and fix our own moral catastrophes, especially those we can't yet see.

Our neurodata can reveal our most private selves. As brain implants become common, how will it be protected?

Christina Maher
University of Sydney

'Hello, world!' In late 2021, these were the first words tweeted by a paralysed man using only his thoughts and a brain–computer interface (BCI) implanted by the company Synchron.

For millions living with paralysis, epilepsy and neuromuscular conditions, BCIs offer restored movement and – a recent development – thought-to-text capabilities. So far, few invasive (implanted) versions of the technology have been commercialised. But a number of companies are determined to change this. Synchron is joined in these efforts by Elon Musk's Neuralink, which has documented a monkey playing the computer game Pong using its BCI, as well as the newer Precision Neuroscience, which recently raised US$41 million towards building a reversible implant thinner than a human hair.

Eventually, BCIs will allow people to carry out a range of tasks using their thoughts. But is this terrific or terrifying?

How do BCIs work?

BCIs can be non-invasive (wearable) or invasive. Electrical activity is the most commonly captured 'neurodata', with invasive BCIs providing better signal quality than non-invasive ones.

The functionality of most BCIs can be summarised as passive, active and reactive. All BCIs use signal processing to filter brain signals. After processing, active and reactive BCIs can return outputs in response to a user's voluntary brain activity. Signals from specific brain regions are considered a combination of many tiny signals from multiple regions.

So BCIs use pattern-recognition algorithms to decipher a signal's potential origins and link it to an intentional event, such as a task or thought.

One of the first implanted BCIs treated drug-resistant seizures in some of the fifty million people with epilepsy. And ongoing clinical trials signal a new era for neurologically and physically impaired people. Outside the clinical realm, however, neurodata exist in a largely unregulated space.

An unknown middleman

In human interaction, thoughts are interpreted by the person experiencing and communicating them, and separately by the person receiving the communication. In this sense, allowing algorithms to interpret our thoughts could be likened to another entity 'speaking' for us. This could raise issues in a future where thought-to-text is widespread.

For example, a BCI may generate the output 'I'm good', when the user intended it to be 'I'm great'. These are similar, but they aren't the same. It's easy enough for an able-bodied person to physically correct the mistake, but for people who can only communicate through BCIs, there's a risk of being misinterpreted.

Moreover, implanted BCIs can provide rich access to all brain signals – there is no option to pick and choose which signals are shared.

Brain data are arguably our most private data because of what can be inferred regarding our identity and mental state. Yet, private BCI companies may not need to inform users about what data are used to train algorithms, or how the data are linked to interpretations that lead to outputs.

In Australia, strict data-storage rules require that all BCI-related patient data are stored on secure servers in a de-identified form, which helps protect patient privacy. But requirements outside of a research context are unclear.

What's at risk if neurodata aren't protected?

BCIs are unlikely to launch us into a dystopian world, in part due to current computational constraints. After all, there's a leap between a BCI sending a short text and interpreting one's entire stream of consciousness. That said, making this leap largely comes down to how well we can train algorithms, which requires more data and computing power. The rise of quantum computing – whenever that may be – could provide these additional computational resources.

Cathy O'Neil's 2016 book *Weapons of Math Destruction* highlights how algorithms that measure complex concepts such as human qualities could let predatory entities make important decisions for the most vulnerable people. Here are some hypothetical worst-case scenarios.

1. Third-party companies might buy neurodata from BCI companies and use it to make decisions, such as whether someone is granted a loan or access to health care.
2. Courts might be allowed to order the neuromonitoring of individuals with the potential to commit crimes, based on their previous history or socio-demographic environment.
3. BCIs specialised for 'neuro-enhancement' could be made a condition of employment, such as in the military. This would blur the boundaries between human reasoning and algorithmic influence.
4. As with all industries where data privacy is critical, there is a genuine risk of neurodata hacking, where cybercriminals access and exploit brain data.

Then there are subtler examples, including the potential for bias. In the future, bias may be introduced into BCI technologies in a number of ways, including through:

- the selection of homogeneous training data
- a lack of diversity among clinical trial participants (especially in control groups)
- a lack of diversity in the teams that design the algorithms and software.

If BCIs are to cater to diverse users, then diversity will need to be factored into every stage of development.

How can we protect neurodata?

The vision for 'neurorights' is an evolving space. The ethical challenges lie in the balance between choosing what is best for individuals and what is best for society at large.

For instance, should individuals in the military be equipped with neuro-enhancing devices so they can better serve their country and protect themselves on the front lines, or would that compromise their individual identity and privacy? And which legislation should capture neurorights: data-protection law, health law, consumer law or criminal law?

In a world first, Chile passed a neurorights law in 2021 to protect mental privacy by explicitly classifying mental data and brain activity as a human right to be legally protected. However, though a step in the right direction, it remains unclear how such a law would be enforced.

One US-based patient group is taking matters into its own hands. The BCI Pioneers is an advocate group ensuring the conversation around neuro-ethics is patient-led. Other efforts include the Neurorights Foundation and the proposal for a 'technocratic oath' modelled on the Hippocratic oath taken by medical doctors. An International Organization for Standardization committee for BCI standards is also underway.

Satellites and space junk may make dark night skies brighter, hindering astronomy and hiding stars from our view

Jessica Heim
University of Southern Queensland

Since time immemorial, humans around the world have looked up in wonder at the night sky. The starry night sky has not only inspired countless works of music, art and poetry, it has also played an important role in time-keeping, navigation and agricultural practices in many traditions.

For many cultures, the night sky, with its planets and stars, and the Milky Way, is considered just as important a part of the natural environment as the forests, lakes and mountains below. Countless people around the world gaze at the night sky – not only amateur and professional astronomers, but also casual observers who enjoy looking up at the stars to contemplate our place in the cosmos.

However, the night sky is changing. Not only is ground-based light pollution rapidly increasing, but growing numbers of satellites and space debris in orbit around Earth are also affecting the night sky.

Earlier research showed that satellites and space debris may increase the overall brightness of the night sky. In a new paper in *Nature Astronomy*, my colleagues and I applied this knowledge to predicting the performance of a major astronomical sky survey. We found this phenomenon may make the survey 7.5 per cent less efficient and US$21.8 million more expensive.

A brighter sky

As a cultural astronomer, I am interested in the role of the night sky in cultural traditions around the world. In particular, I am interested in how light pollution and increasing satellite numbers affect different communities.

The number of satellites in orbit is growing rapidly. Since 2019, the number of functional satellites in orbit has more than doubled to around 7600. The increase is mostly due to SpaceX and other companies launching large groups of satellites to provide high-speed internet communications around the world.

By the end of this decade, we estimate there may be 100,000 satellites in orbit around Earth. Collisions that generate space debris are more likely as space fills with new satellites. Other sources of debris include the intentional destruction of satellites in space warfare tests.

Increasing numbers of satellites and amounts of space debris reflect ever more sunlight towards the night side of Earth. This will almost certainly change the appearance of the night sky and make it harder for astronomers to do research.

One way satellites affect astronomy is by appearing as moving points of light, which show up as streaks across astronomers' images. Another is by increasing diffuse night sky brightness. This means all the satellites that are too dim or small to be seen individually, as well as all the small bits of space debris, still reflect sunlight, and their collective effect is to make the night sky appear less dark.

Hard times for astronomers

In our research, we present the first published calculations of the aggregate effects of satellites and space debris in low-Earth orbit on major ground-based astronomy research facilities.

We looked at the effect on the planned large-scale survey of the night sky to be carried out at the Vera Rubin Observatory in northern Chile, starting in 2024. We found that, by 2030, reflected light from objects in low-Earth orbit will likely increase the diffuse background brightness for this survey by at least 7.5 per cent compared to an unpolluted sky. This would diminish the efficiency of this survey by 7.5 per cent as well. Over the ten-year lifetime of the survey, we estimate this would add some US$21.8 million to the total project cost.

Brighter night skies mean longer exposures through telescopes are needed to see distant objects in the cosmos. This will mean that, for projects with a fixed amount of observing time, less science will be accomplished, and there will be increased competition for telescope access. In addition, brighter night skies will reduce the detection limits of sky surveys, and dimmer objects may not be detected, resulting in missed research opportunities.

Some astrophysical events are rare, and if researchers are unable to view them when they occur, there might not be an opportunity to easily see a given event again during a survey's operational period. One example of faint objects is near-Earth objects – comets and asteroids in orbits close to Earth. Brighter night skies make it more likely such potentially hazardous objects may remain undetected.

A dramatic and unprecedented transformation

Increases in diffuse night sky brightness will also change how we see the night sky with the unaided eye. As the human eye cannot resolve individual small objects as well as a telescope can, a proliferation of satellites and space debris will create an even greater increase in the apparent brightness of the night sky. (When using a telescope or binoculars, one would be able to make out more of the dimmer satellites individually.)

The projected increase in night sky brightness will make it more difficult to see fainter stars and the Milky Way, both of which are important in various cultural traditions. Unlike 'ground-based' light pollution, which tends to be the worst near large cities and heavily populated areas, the changes to the sky will be visible from essentially everywhere on Earth's surface.

Our models give us a conservative lower limit for a likely increase in night sky brightness. If the amount of satellites and space debris continues to grow at the expected rate, the impacts will be even more pronounced.

As we note in our paper, 'We are witnessing a dramatic, fundamental, and perhaps semi-permanent transformation of the night sky without historical precedent and with limited oversight'. Such a transformation will have profound consequences for professional astronomy as well as for anyone who wishes to view an unpolluted night sky.

Indigenous knowledge is increasingly valued, but to fully respect it we need to decolonise science. Here's how

Te Kahuratai Moko-Painting
University of Auckland

Tara McAllister
Victoria University of Wellington

We are witnessing a resurgence of indigenous knowledge and a growing acknowledgement of its scientific value worldwide.

In Aotearoa, there has been some progress, including the introduction of a public holiday to mark Matariki, the beginning of a new year in maramataka – the Māori calendar based on the phases of the Moon, the movement of stars and the timing of ecological changes. But this progress has not been straightforward, with some scientists publicly questioning the scientific value of mātauranga (Māori knowledge and knowledge system). At the same time, Māori scientists have drawn on and advanced mātauranga and continue to make space for te reo (Māori language), tikanga (Māori customary system of values and practices) and honouring Te Tiriti o Waitangi in research.

Our April 2023 publication explores pūtaiao – a way of conducting research grounded in kaupapa (matter of discussion) Māori. In education, pūtaiao is often simplified to mean science taught in Māori-medium schools that includes mātauranga, or science taught in te reo more broadly. But science based on kaupapa Māori is generally by Māori, for Māori and with Māori.

Our research extends kaupapa Māori (a philosophical doctrine, incorporating the knowledge, skills, attitudes and values of Māori society) and the important work of pūtaiao in schools into tertiary scientific research. We envision pūtaiao as a way of doing science that is led by Māori and firmly positioned in te ao Māori (including mātauranga, te reo and tikanga).

Pūtaiao as decolonising science

Pūtaiao privileges Māori ways of knowing, being and doing. It is a political speaking-back for the inclusion of te ao Māori – mātauranga, te reo, tikanga and Te Tiriti o Waitangi – in science.

Conducting research in this way is not new. Many Māori scientists have drawn on mātauranga and kaupapa Māori in their research for decades. Our conceptualisation of pūtaiao is an affirmation of the work of Māori scientists and a pathway for redefining and transforming scientific research for future generations.

Decolonising science is at the heart of pūtaiao. It challenges and critiques the academy and disciplines of Western science. Decolonising science requires a focus on histories, structures and institutions that act as barriers to mātauranga, te reo and tikanga. We argue that decolonising science is a necessary step before we can indigenise science.

Like mātauranga, pūtaiao is embedded in place and in the people of those places. It centres, prioritises and affirms Māori identity in the context of scientific research and science identity.

The importance of the researcher in pūtaiao

How we identify as Māori – tangata whenua or rāwaho (people not related to the hapū or whānau), ahi kā (people who keep the home fires burning) or ahi mātaotao (people who may have been disconnected to the land through lack of occupation over generations) – fundamentally changes how we interact with people and place through research. To practise pūtaiao effectively, researchers are required to understand who they are and how that informs the research questions asked, the research relationships formed, the location of the research and the way research is conducted.

Kaupapa Māori, as articulated by distinguished education scholar Graham Hingangaroa Smith, requires two approaches to decolonisation: culturalist and structuralist.

Culturalist approaches centre te reo, mātauranga and tikanga. The groundbreaking work led by professor of marine science and aquaculture Kura Paul-Burke, using mātauranga to enhance shellfish restoration, is an excellent example of a culturalist approach to decolonising science.

A structuralist approach means paying attention to and dismantling the structures within science which continue to exclude Māori knowledge and people. It encourages us to think about the colonial roots of science and how science has been used to justify colonial violence and oppression of Māori.

Captain Cook's 'scientific voyage' to Aotearoa is a great example of how colonisation occurred under the guise of science.

Challenging the status quo

Pūtaiao reframes the conversation around the inclusion of mātauranga Māori in science. It considers the relationship between te ao Māori, the researcher and science to imagine how to decolonise, indigenise and transform science. We understand science not simply as scientific knowledge but as a knowledge system that spans research, education, academia, scientific practice and publications – as well as the evaluation and funding of, and access to, science, its legitimacy and its relationship to policy and government.

There has been much research on Māori experiences within the science system, including the cultural double shift when Māori scientists are expected to lift their colleagues' understanding, racism and the difficulties of inclusion. A lone Māori scientist is often tasked with upskilling his or her colleagues, representing Māori on committees and leading cultural practices, in addition to standard loads of supervising, teaching and research.

To challenge the status quo, we explored different ways of creating ecosystems or 'flourishing forests' of Māori scientists to advance pūtaiao. This includes creating networks of Māori staff in science by establishing research centres such as Te Pūtahi o Pūtaiao and the Centre of Indigenous Science. It also means creating research projects that move beyond the siloed disciplines within the science system. In this way, pūtaiao enables Māori to see themselves and be seen within science.

Pūtaiao offers a practical foundation, connecting Māori science leaders to transform science. Whether this happens through new university courses, academic programs, research centres, institutions or regional and community hubs remains to be seen.

It is certain, however, that pūtaiao, conceptualised as kaupapa Māori science, offers many pathways for Māori scientists to continue to draw on and advance more than mātauranga to decolonise and, ultimately, redefine science into the future.

PART V

Protecting our fragile world

Thinking of having a baby as the planet collapses? First, ask yourself five big ethical questions

Craig Stanbury
Monash University

Do you want to have a baby? But, on a planet rocked by the climate crisis, ecosystem collapse, famine and poverty, is having one just adding to the problem, and therefore unethical?

I am a PhD candidate at Monash Bioethics Centre, and I research the ethics of procreation in a time of climate change. I've found there's no simple 'yes' or 'no' answer to whether we should produce more children when Earth is in such dire straits.

People who want to have children are faced with a dilemma. Creating a child who will be responsible for high emissions over their lifetime requires others to stay in poverty – if the planet is to operate within its physical limits. This, it can easily be argued, furthers injustice and inequality. But many of us want to have children. Doing so can be one of the most meaningful things we do with our life.

What should we do? Ethics can provide an answer. It shows there is a moral obligation to consider the effects of child-bearing without obliging people to not have children as a result.

What is overpopulation?

Many people argue the world has an overpopulation problem. Overpopulation has been defined as the state where there are more people than can live on Earth in comfort, happiness and health and still leave the world a fit place for future generations. But this definition is open to interpretation. Overpopulation is not just about numbers but also values. If people in affluent countries value their lifestyles – and the opportunity for others to have the same lifestyle – then the world is overpopulated.

I live in inner-city Melbourne. When I calculate my ecological footprint, it's confronting to discover we would need about four Earths for everyone to live like me. If everyone lived like the average American, we would need more than five Earths.

Indeed, estimates by ecologists and philosophers show a person born in the developed world can enjoy their lifestyle only if there are no more than two or three billion people on the planet. There are now more than eight billion.

We could address the dilemma by decreasing per-capita emissions of greenhouse gases. However, this on its own won't be sufficient. Why?

First, it's difficult to reduce emissions at the speed required to mitigate catastrophic climate change. The goal of the Paris Agreement is to prevent the world from warming by 2 degrees Celsius from pre-industrial levels. To achieve this goal, we must halve emissions by 2030, halve them again by 2040, and again by 2050.

Unfortunately, we are not on track to achieve the Paris goals. This failure will cause significant suffering and millions of deaths. And the most disadvantaged people will be affected first and most severely. This is unjust.

Second, developing countries must be allowed to increase their emissions to escape poverty. People in poverty consume very few resources. To stay at this low level of consumption is dehumanising. We should be advocating for many people to consume more.

Third, even if the world's average per capita emissions decrease, a growing population multiplies emissions. For instance, if global fertility rates dropped by only 0.5 births per woman, about 5.1 billion tonnes of carbon would be saved each year by the end of the century. This would contribute to between 16 per cent and 29 per cent of the emissions savings needed to avoid catastrophic climate change.

However, emissions tend to grow on a one-to-one ratio with rising populations. Between 1975 and 2009, for example, both population and emissions rose by 43 per cent in the United States. Failing to address population growth means we may undo the good work achieved by reducing per-capita emissions.

And finally, we cannot address per-capita emissions without addressing reproduction. The decision to not bring someone into the world is about twenty times more effective at reducing individual emissions than the sum total of many other 'green' acts we can do, such as recycling and driving less.

For instance, in a developed nation, having one fewer child saves about 58 tonnes of emissions per year. The next-best decision someone can make to limit their emissions is to live car-free. But this will only save about 2.4 tonnes of emissions per year.

As ethicists have recently pointed out, if there is any duty to reduce our per-capita emissions, there is a duty to limit the amount of children we have.

Resolving the dilemma

I should acknowledge here that I don't have the lived experience of being a woman or person who can carry a child, nor do I have children yet. However, I do believe the world must address overpopulation.

I say this knowing it is not an easy or a comfortable topic to broach. It involves sexuality and contraception, personal rights and religion. And I realise there is no way forward that can solve all injustices.

If people in affluent nations keep bringing children into the world, there will not be enough resources for many current and future people to live and flourish. But it would also be unjust to demand an individual give up reproducing. The freedom to decide whether to bring someone into the world is central to many people's dignity and life's meaning. And the United Nations Declaration of Human Rights recognises that every man and woman has the right to found a family.

So, the most appropriate answer is not one that seeks to eliminate injustices altogether. Rather, it should minimise injustice as much as possible.

Telling people not to have children, or to have fewer children, is too strong. The solution must tread a finer line. But how? By placing a moral obligation on people to consider the environmental and justice issues of bringing someone into the world.

Five big questions

For a person wanting children, this means it's no longer enough to only ask questions such as: can I be a good parent? Do I have the means to support a child? Anyone with the means to control their fertility now has an obligation to also ask themselves the following five questions:

1. Will my child have a high-emissions lifestyle and will this mean others must live in poverty? If so, is this justifiable?
2. Do I have biological parenting desires; that is, the desire to parent someone who has my genes? Or do I simply have parenting desires;

that is, the desire to raise someone in a loving environment according to my values, regardless of their genes?

3. Even if I might discover a strong biological connection once I have a child, could I be fulfilled in my life if I raised someone who is not biologically connected to me?
4. If I have only parenting desires, can this be satisfied in other ways, such as through fostering, teaching, mentoring or, if possible, adopting?
5. Does satisfying my parenting desires in another way particularly apply to me if I already have one biological child?

Often, people who choose not to have children feel the need to explain the decision to others. The above approach would mean the reverse: it requires that people who wish to ethically bring someone into the world must themselves address difficult questions.

A just society values everyone being able to pursue having a child if they wish to. Yet, it also demands that everyone consider the ramifications of doing so.

Australia's 116 new coal, oil and gas projects equate to 215 new coal power stations

Richard Denniss
Australian National University

Australia has 116 new coal, oil and gas projects in the pipeline. If they all proceed as planned, an extra 1.4 billion tonnes of greenhouse gases will be released into the atmosphere annually by 2030.

To put that in perspective, Australia's total domestic greenhouse gas emissions in 2021–22 were 490 million tonnes. So, annual emissions from these new projects will be almost three times larger than the nation's 2021–22 emissions. That's the equivalent of starting up 215 new coal power stations, based on the average emissions of Australia's existing coal power stations.

The reason we can get away with this is that the current global framework for emissions accounting only considers emissions generated onshore. And almost all coal, oil and gas from these new projects would be exported. But as we share the atmosphere with the rest of the people on the planet, the consequences will come back to bite us.

The 2023 *Synthesis Report* from the Intergovernmental Panel on Climate Change (IPCC) described how fossil fuels are wreaking havoc on the planet. The science is clear: the IPCC says fossil fuel use is overwhelmingly driving global warming. 'The sooner emissions are reduced this decade, the greater our chance of limiting warming to 1.5°C or 2°C. Projected CO_2 emissions from existing fossil fuel infrastructure (power plants, mines, pipelines) without additional abatement exceed the remaining carbon budget for 1.5°C,' says the IPCC, let alone new coal, oil and gas projects.

In the words of UN Secretary-General António Guterres: 'Every country must be part of the solution. Demanding others move first only ensures humanity comes last.'

Guterres added that 'the acceleration agenda calls for a number of other actions', specifically:

- no new coal, and the phasing out of coal by 2030 in OECD countries and by 2040 in all other countries
- ending all international public and private funding of coal
- ensuring net-zero electricity generation by 2035 for all developed countries and by 2040 for the rest of the world
- ceasing all licensing or funding of new oil and gas – consistent with the findings of the International Energy Agency (IEA)
- stopping any expansion of existing oil and gas reserves
- shifting subsidies from fossil fuels to a just-energy transition
- establishing a global phase-down of existing oil and gas production compatible with the 2050 global net-zero target.

Hidden in plain sight

Our research, released in March by the Australia Institute, reveals the pollution from Australia's 116 new fossil fuel projects. These are listed among the federal government's major projects. Government analysts estimate each project's start date and annual production figures. If they are correct, by 2030 the projects will produce a total of 1466 million tonnes of coal and 15,400 petajoules of gas and oil.

New or planned fossil fuel resource projects

New gas, oil and coal projects through to 2030, by type and size of project, Australia.

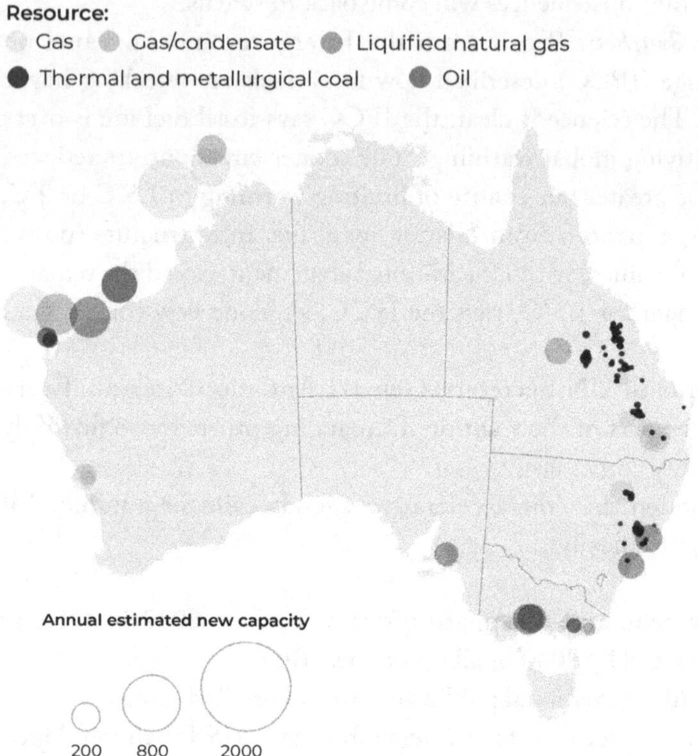

Source: Office of the Chief Economist. Created with Datawrapper.

Then it's fairly straightforward to calculate emissions. We simply multiplied these enormous new fossil fuel volumes by their 'emissions factors'. When 1 tonne of coal is burned, it releases approximately 2.65 tonnes of carbon dioxide or its equivalent (CO_2-e) into the atmosphere, and burning 1 terajoule (0.001 petajoules) of natural gas results in 51.5 tonnes of CO_2-e. Combined with the 164 million tonnes of emissions that the mining of these fuels would cause, the result is a planet-warming, but spine-chilling, total of 4.8 billion tonnes by 2030.

This amount is twenty-four times greater than the ambition of the federal government's key emissions reduction policy, the so-called Safeguard Mechanism (SGM). That aims to reduce emissions by 205 million tonnes over the same period.

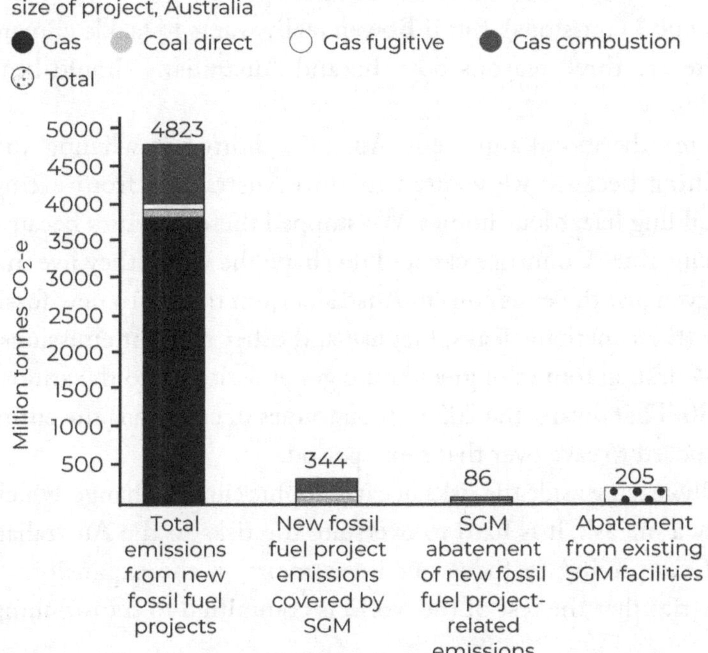

Source: Author's calculations based on Department of Industry, Science and Resources 2022.

Rather than embrace the task of decarbonising the Australian economy, the Albanese government has continued down the path laid out by the former Coalition government. It's a path that relies more heavily on the use of carbon offsets than curtailing coal and gas.

Even though the rest of the world is committed to burning less fossil fuels, there are more gas and coalmine project proposals in Australia today than there were in 2021. Note also that this list does not include several large, advanced projects actively supported by Australian governments, including Santos' Barossa gas field, Shell's Bowen Gas Project, Chevron's Clio-Acme, and several vast, new, unconventional gas basins, including the Beetaloo, Canning and Lake Eyre basins.

Three reasons to change our ways

Climate change minister Chris Bowen argues that Australians are not responsible for the emissions from our fossil fuel exports. That's because the international accounting rules distinguish between the emissions that occur within our borders (known as scope 1 and 2 emissions) and those that occur when other countries burn the coal and gas we sell them (known as scope 3 emissions). But if Bowen really wants to tackle climate change, there are three reasons both he and Australians should bear this responsibility.

First, there's the moral argument. Australia didn't ban whaling and asbestos mining because we wanted to stop Australians from eating whales or building hazardous homes. We stopped these activities because they were dangerous. Countries can and do shape the world they live in.

Second, even just the emissions in Australia from these 116 new fossil fuel projects (their methane leaks, fuel use and other relevant emissions) will pour 344 million tonnes of greenhouse gas emissions into the atmosphere by 2030. That dwarfs the 205 million tonnes of emissions the entire SGM is supposed to save over that same period.

And finally, leaving aside the risks of catastrophic climate change, which is admittedly a big ask, it is hard to overstate the risks to the Australian economy of continuing to focus our investment on the expansion of export industries that the rest of the world is committed to transitioning away from.

If we aimed the $11 billion per year we spend on fossil fuel subsidies at decarbonising our economy, we would slash emissions in no time.

No new coal, oil and gas

The Australian Government continues to support unlimited growth in fossil fuel production and export, despite clear statements from the UN, the IEA and the IPCC that new fossil fuel projects are incompatible with global temperature goals.

No matter where in the world Australian fossil fuels are burned, they will turn up the heat. We can't escape the simple truth that humanity must stop burning fossil fuels. It's the only path to a liveable future.

Torrents of Antarctic meltwater are slowing the currents that drive our vital ocean 'overturning' – and threaten its collapse

Matthew England
UNSW Sydney

Adele Morrison
Australian National University

Andy Hogg
Australian National University

Qian Li
Massachusetts Institute of Technology

Steve Rintoul
CSIRO

Off the coast of Antarctica, trillions of tonnes of cold, salty water sink to great depths. As the water sinks, it drives the deepest flows of the 'overturning' circulation – a network of strong currents spanning the world's oceans. The overturning circulation carries heat, carbon, oxygen and nutrients around the globe, and fundamentally influences climate, sea levels and the productivity of marine ecosystems.

But there are worrying signs these currents are slowing down. They may even collapse. If this happens, it would deprive the deep ocean of oxygen, limit the return of nutrients back to the sea surface, and potentially cause further melt-back of ice as water near the ice shelves warms in response. There would be major global ramifications for ocean ecosystems, climate and sea-level rise.

Our research, published this year in the journal *Nature*, uses new ocean model projections to look at changes in the deep ocean out to the year 2050. Our projections show a slowing of the Antarctic overturning circulation and deep ocean warming over the next few decades. Physical measurements confirm these changes are already well underway.

Climate change is to blame. As Antarctica melts, more freshwater flows into the oceans. This disrupts the sinking of cold, salty, oxygen-rich water to the bottom of the ocean. From there, this water normally spreads northwards to ventilate the far reaches of the deep Indian, Pacific and Atlantic oceans. But that could all come to an end soon. In our lifetimes.

Why does this matter?

As part of this overturning, about 250 trillion tonnes of icy cold Antarctic surface water sinks into the ocean abyss each year. The sinking near Antarctica is balanced by upwelling at other latitudes. The resulting overturning circulation carries oxygen to the deep ocean and eventually returns nutrients to the sea surface, where they are available to support marine life.

If the Antarctic overturning slows down, nutrient-rich sea water will build up on the seabed, 5 kilometres below the surface. These nutrients will be lost to marine ecosystems at or near the surface, damaging fisheries.

Changes in the overturning circulation could also mean more heat gets to the ice, particularly around West Antarctica, the area with the greatest rate of ice-mass loss over the past few decades. This would accelerate global sea-level rise.

An overturning slowdown would also reduce the ocean's ability to take up carbon dioxide, leaving more greenhouse gas emissions in the atmosphere. And more greenhouse gases means more warming, making matters worse.

Meltwater-induced weakening of the Antarctic overturning circulation could also shift tropical rainfall bands around a thousand kilometres to the north.

Put simply, a slowing or collapse of the overturning circulation would change our climate and marine environment in profound and potentially irreversible ways.

Signs of worrying change

The remote reaches of the oceans that surround Antarctica are some of the toughest regions to plan and undertake field campaigns. Voyages are long, weather can be brutal and sea ice limits access for much of the year. This means there are few measurements to track how the Antarctic margin is changing. But where sufficient data exist, we can see clear signs of increased transport of warm waters towards Antarctica, which in turn causes ice melt at key locations.

Indeed, the signs of melting around the edges of Antarctica are very clear, with increasingly large volumes of freshwater flowing into the ocean and making nearby waters less salty and therefore less dense. And that's all that's needed to slow the overturning circulation. Denser water sinks; lighter water does not.

How did we find this out?

Apart from sparse measurements, incomplete models have limited our understanding of ocean circulation around Antarctica. For example, the latest set of global coupled model projections analysed by the IPCC exhibits biases in the region. This limits the ability of these models in projecting the future fate of the Antarctic overturning circulation.

To explore future changes, we took a high-resolution global ocean model that realistically represents the formation and sinking of dense water near Antarctica. We ran three different experiments: one where conditions remained unchanged from the 1990s; a second forced by projected changes in temperature and wind; and a third also including projected changes in meltwater from Antarctica and Greenland. In this way, we could separate the effects of changes in winds and warming from changes due to ice melt.

The findings were striking. The model projects the overturning circulation around Antarctica will slow by more than 40 per cent over the next three decades, driven almost entirely by pulses of meltwater. Over the same period, our modelling also predicts a 20 per cent weakening of the famous North Atlantic overturning circulation which keeps Europe's climate mild. Both changes would dramatically reduce the renewal and overturning of the ocean interior.

We've long known the North Atlantic overturning currents are vulnerable, with observations suggesting a slowdown is already well underway, and projections of a tipping point coming soon. Our results suggest Antarctica looks poised to match its Northern Hemisphere counterpart – and then some.

What next?

Much of the abyssal ocean has warmed in recent decades, with the most rapid trends detected near Antarctica, in a pattern very similar to our model simulations. Our projections extend out only to 2050. Beyond 2050, in the absence of strong emissions reductions, the climate will continue to warm and the ice sheets will continue to melt. If so, we anticipate the Southern Ocean overturning will continue to slow to the end of the century and beyond.

The projected slowdown of Antarctic overturning is a direct response to input of freshwater from melting ice. Meltwater flows are directly linked to how much the planet warms, which in turn depends on the greenhouse gases we emit.

Our study shows continuing ice melt will not only raise sea levels, but also change the massive overturning circulation currents which can drive further ice melt and hence more sea-level rise, and damage climate and ecosystems worldwide. It's yet another reason to address the climate crisis – and fast.

Australia is facing a 450,000-tonne mountain of used solar panels. Here's how to turn it into a valuable asset

Archie Chapman
University of Queensland

There were an estimated 100 million individual solar photovoltaic (PV) panels in Australia at the end of 2022. We estimate this number will likely grow to over two billion if we are to meet Australia's 2050 net-zero emissions target. This growth means Australia will face a 450,000-tonne mountain of used PV panels by 2040.

Managing all those discarded PV panels will be a huge job. Rather than being treated as 'waste', though, these panels could be a source of social, environmental and economic value. Our industry report outlines how we can realise that value.

PV panels contain a variety of valuable materials. The panels can also be put to new uses, such as on uninhabited community and sports club buildings, or applied to agricultural irrigation pumps, or used for camping and caravanning. However, at present, they tend to follow a linear 'take, make, dispose' life cycle. This results in many PV panels being sent to landfill or stockpiled. Much of their value is wasted.

What did the research look at?

The University of Queensland and Circular PV Alliance have assessed the market for used and surplus PV panels, with funding from Energy Consumers Australia. Our goal was to understand potential customers and value streams for used PV panels. We also wished to identify market or policy barriers to reusing, repurposing and recycling these panels.

We reviewed the academic research on the topic and conducted a series of interviews. Thirteen organisations with diverse interests in solar energy and PV panel re-use and recycling participated. A series of recurrent themes emerged that indicate potential or perceived opportunities and challenges for PV panel re-use.

What did the research find?

Overall, there was broad concern among interviewees that PV panels are being decommissioned before the end of their productive lives. A few key reasons stood out:

- Renewable energy certificates encourage PV investors to install new panels rather than extend the life of older panels, because the subsidy is paid in full on installation, rather than as power is generated.
- Low-quality PV products have a high failure rate.
- An array that combines different PV panels can be limited by the lowest-performing panel.

These issues contribute to the already large amounts of discarded panels coming from solar farms, and warranty and insurance claims. However, we also found that reclaimed PV panels offer low-cost, clean-energy options for households and community energy projects.

Even when not re-usable, PV panels include valuable materials that can be recovered. The average silicon panel contains silver (47 per cent of recycled materials value), aluminium (frame, 26 per cent), silicon (cells, 11 per cent), glass (8 per cent) and copper (8 per cent).

And PV panel recycling is becoming more efficient. This has led to better-quality outputs and higher recovery rates. For example, nano-silicon created by processing recovered silicon can sell for over $44,000 per kilogram.

A shift towards viewing a PV panel as a valuable resource or asset, rather than 'waste', will improve both consumer and industry understanding of its inherent value, even when it's not brand new.

How do we turn 'waste' into an asset?

We can keep used PV panels out of landfill by treating them as an asset through a value-capture system. This will create a variety of benefits and opportunities.

The circular economy model loops the 'take, make, re-use' phases into a self-sustaining cycle. It provides a foundation to grow markets for used PV panels. This will tap into consumer demands for credible and sustainable products and services.

There are already successful examples of similar solutions for other products in Australia and around the world. Australian examples include the National Television and Computer Recycling Scheme and Tyre Stewardship Australia, as well as state-based beverage container deposit schemes.

So, how do we set up a circular economy for PV panels? We found a combination of policies, regulations and commercial services can overcome the obstacles to re-use and recycling.

A consistent, national approach is needed to establish successful markets for used PV panels. Standards for testing and certifying these panels, as well as repair warranties, are essential to build consumer trust in this product.

Industry reporting and accreditation requirements as well as product traceability, so the re-used and recycled panels can be accounted for, are all important elements of product stewardship and used PV panel markets.

Targeted engagement with a broader range of potential consumers, insurers and PV panel manufacturers will help overcome the perceived barriers to re-using panels.

Taken together, these actions are the building blocks for creating a circular economy for PV panels in Australia. The looming volumes of used panels and ever-increasing amount of solar energy being installed in Australia compel us to do this. Consumers, industry and the environment will all benefit.

Editor's note: The author acknowledges Megan Jones, Circular PV Alliance co-founder and director, for her contribution to this article.

After the chainsaws, the quiet: Victoria's rapid exit from native forest logging is welcome – and long overdue

David Lindenmayer
Australian National University
Chris Taylor
Australian National University

By the end of this year, Victoria's trouble-plagued native forest industry will end – six years ahead of schedule. The state's iconic mountain ash forests and endangered wildlife will at last be safe from chainsaws. And there will be no shortage of wood. There's more than enough plantation timber to fill the gap.

This is excellent news for forests, the state's economy and its threatened species. We congratulate the Victorian Government for this decision.

Ending native forest logging is long overdue. For decades, we've known how much damage it does to biodiversity. The logging of vast areas of Victoria's native forests over the past few decades has pushed many once-common animals, such as the greater glider, to become endangered. Even now, the last remaining logging areas proposed under the state's Timber Release Plan overlap directly with the areas of highest conservation value for biodiversity.

Our research has catalogued the damage done to produce low-value products such as woodchips and paper pulp. The industry never made economic sense. The state-owned logging company, VicForests, has been running at a loss for many years. The industry can switch to our abundant plantations of eucalyptus and pine.

What damage did native forest logging do?

The vast majority of areas slated for logging provide habitat for more than fifty threatened and rare species. We know that the more forests are logged, the less likely we are to find species such as the critically endangered Leadbeater's Possum. Logging pushes species into decline. Common species become threatened and threatened species move closer to extinction.

The lead author of this article has been part of a team conducting ecological monitoring and research in Victoria's forests for almost forty years. We have seen the damage first-hand.

We've watched old forests of high conservation value be clear-felled when they should not have been. We've watched essential habitat such as large old trees, with their all-important nesting hollows, become rarer and rarer.

We have seen extraordinary animals such as the Southern Greater Glider go from the most common species identified in night surveys to being so scarce they're now endangered.

We have seen once-intact landscapes become dominated by highly flammable young forest at risk of extremely severe wildfires.

And we have watched in dismay as logging has fragmented the landscape. Now, up to 70 per cent of Victoria's critically endangered mountain ash forests are either severely disturbed by wildfire and logging or are within 200 metres of such areas.

Native forest logging never made sense

Almost all (86 per cent) of felled native forests in Victoria are turned into low-value products such as woodchips, paper pulp and boxliners. In 2018, we estimated sawn timber equated to just 14 per cent of the volume of logs cut from native forests. By contrast, more than 80 per cent of all sawn timber in Victoria comes from plantations. Native forest timber does not help build houses.

Bringing forward the end of native forest logging from 2030 will be a major boost for climate action – equal to removing 730,000 petrol or diesel cars from our roads every year. This single decision gives Victoria – and Australia – a far greater chance of meeting emissions reductions targets.

In its last annual report, VicForests announced a loss of $54 million and a loan of $80 million. It's now propped up only by the Victorian Treasury. Even before these losses, the Victorian Parliamentary Budget Office showed the state would be $190 million better off without it.

How can we help forests recover?

Ending logging will take pressure off our forests. But we can't simply walk away from heavily damaged areas. Many areas have never properly regenerated after logging or repeated fires.

In northeastern Victoria, years of logging have warped the composition of tree species in the forest; many areas are dominated by trees that are largely unsuitable as food sources for koalas and greater gliders.

The urgent task is to restore forests across Victoria while managing fire and invasive species such as deer.

That's not all. We will still need wood and paper. Ending native forest logging requires getting things right in Australia's plantations.

At present, we export up to 95 per cent of all plantation eucalypt logs we grow for processing overseas. That's a missed opportunity for local jobs. Even now, the plantation sector is crying out for more workers in haulage and processing. This sector offers comparable jobs for workers leaving the native forest sector. But there will be other jobs: forest restoration, firefighting, feral animal control, carbon stock management and more. Getting the transition right is important.

The exit from native forest logging must now be coupled with the declaration of a Great Forest National Park in the Central Highlands region, which has been a hotspot for native forest logging in recent decades. It's been almost ten years since the state's then-environment minister Lisa Neville promised this park would be declared. Once established, the new park should be co-managed with First Nations people to ensure Aboriginal self-determination, as well as good opportunities to work on Country.

Today is a day for celebrating. At last, Victoria's government has acted for the future. Preserving our native forests is worth much more in carbon storage, water production and tourism than they ever were as woodchips.

Victoria's move is a clarion call to other Australian states still doggedly logging their precious forests.

PART VI

Improving our health and wellbeing

Ozempic helps weight loss by making you feel full. But certain foods can do the same thing – without the side effects

Emma Beckett
University of Newcastle

You've probably heard about the medication Ozempic, used to manage type 2 diabetes and as a weight-loss drug. Ozempic (and the similar drug Wegovy) has had more than its fair share of headlines and controversies – a global supply shortage, tweets about using it from Elon Musk, approval for adolescent weight loss in the United States. Oscars host Jimmy Kimmel even joked about it on film's night of nights this year.

But how much do we really need drugs like Ozempic? Can we use food as medicine to replace them?

How does Ozempic work?

The active ingredient in Ozempic is semaglutide, which works by inducing satiety. This feeling of being satisfied, or 'full', suppresses appetite. This is why it works for weight loss. Semaglutide also helps the pancreas produce insulin, which is how it helps manage type 2 diabetes. Our body needs insulin to move the glucose (or blood sugar) we get from food inside cells, so we can use it as energy.

Semaglutide works by mimicking the role of a natural hormone, called GLP-1 (glucagon-like peptide-1), which is normally produced in response to detecting nutrients when we eat. GLP-1 is part of the signalling pathway that tells your body you have eaten, and prepares it to use the energy that comes from your food.

Can food do that?

The nutrients that trigger GLP-1 secretion are macronutrients – simple sugars (monosaccharides), peptides and amino acids (from proteins), and short-chain fatty acids (from fats and also produced by good gut bacteria). There are lots of these macronutrients in energy-dense foods, which tend to be foods high in fat or sugars and with a low water content. There is evidence that by choosing foods high in these nutrients, GLP-1 levels can be increased.

This means a healthy diet, high in GLP-1-stimulating nutrients, can increase GLP-1 levels. This could be foods with good fats, such as avocado or nuts, or lean protein sources such as eggs. And foods high in fermentable fibres, such as vegetables and whole grains, feed our gut bacteria, which then produce short-chain fatty acids able to trigger GLP-1 secretion.

This is why high-fat, high-fibre and high-protein diets can all help you feel fuller for longer. It's also why diet change is part of both weight and type 2 diabetes management.

Not so fast ...

However, it's not necessarily that simple for everyone. This system also means that when we diet, and restrict energy intake, we get more hungry. And for some people, that 'set point' for weight and hunger might be different.

Some studies have shown GLP-1 levels, particularly after meals, are lower in people with obesity. This could be from reduced production of GLP-1, or increased breakdown. The receptors that detect it might also be less sensitive or there might be fewer receptors. This could be because of differences in the genes that code for GLP-1, the receptors or parts of the pathways that regulate production. These genetic differences are things we can't change.

So, are injections the easier fix?

While diet and drugs can both work, both have their challenges.

Medications like Ozempic can have side effects, including nausea, vomiting, diarrhoea and issues in other organs. Plus, when you stop taking it, the feelings of suppressed appetite will start to go away, and people will start to feel hungry at their old levels. If you've lost lots of weight quickly, you may feel even hungrier than before.

Dietary changes have much fewer risks in terms of side effects, but the responses will take more time and effort. In our busy modern society, costs, time, skills, accessibility and other pressures can also be barriers to healthy eating, feeling full and insulin levels.

Dietary and medication solutions often put the focus on the individual making changes to improve health outcomes, but systemic changes that reduce the pressures and barriers that make healthy eating hard (such as shortening work weeks or raising the minimum wage), are much more likely to make a difference.

It's also important to remember that weight is only one part of the health equation. If you suppress your appetite but maintain a diet high in ultra-processed foods and low in micronutrients, you could lose weight but not increase your actual nourishment. So, support to improve dietary choices is needed, regardless of medication use or weight loss, for true health improvements.

The bottom line

The old quote 'Let food be thy medicine' is catchy and often based on science, especially when drugs are deliberately chosen or designed to mimic hormones and compounds already naturally occurring in the body. Changing diet is a way to modify our health and our biological responses. But these effects occur on a background of our personal biology and our unique life circumstances.

For some people, medication will be a tool to improve weight and insulin-related outcomes. For others, food alone is a reasonable pathway to success.

While the science is for populations, health care is individual, and decisions around food and/or medicine should be made with the considered advice of healthcare professionals. General practitioners and dietitians can work with your individual situation and needs.

We worked out how many tobacco lobbyists end up in government, and vice versa. It's a lot

Becky Freeman
University of Sydney
Christina Watts
University of Sydney

This year, we revealed the extent of the close relationship between tobacco lobbyists and government, in the first Australian study of its kind. Our study found about half of people involved in tobacco lobbying held positions in Australian governments before or after working for the tobacco industry.

This 'revolving door' between tobacco lobbyists and government is a key political lobbying mechanism to influence public health policy. So, we urgently need to strengthen the rules and legislation around lobbying if we are to avoid industry influencing policies on issues such as tobacco control and vaping.

What we did and what we found

We gathered information from sources including federal, state and territory government lobbyist registers, the social networking platform LinkedIn, and Australian news media. We identified fifty-six lobbyists representing tobacco companies (via lobbyist registers and archives) and another seventy-three current and former in-house tobacco lobbyists (via other means).

We found 48 per cent of in-house tobacco company lobbyists and 55 per cent of lobbyists acting on behalf of tobacco companies held positions in Australian state or federal governments before or after working for the tobacco industry. Senior government roles included members of parliament, senators, chief or deputy chiefs of staff and senior ministerial advisers. Around half of the lobbyists had moved into or out of their government roles within a year of working for a tobacco company (56 per cent) or as a lobbyist for one (48 per cent).

We also documented how tobacco companies use third-party allies to indirectly lobby government – a form of lobbying that is poorly recorded on lobbyist registers and is not easily tracked. For example, the Australian Retail Vaping Industry Association was created with funding from global tobacco company Philip Morris International and lobbied to weaken Australian vaping regulations.

Why is this a worry?

We've long suspected there has been a revolving door between government and the tobacco industry, whereby tobacco companies recruit people who have previously held senior government roles to lobby for them. It's a tactic common in the gambling, alcohol and food industries. The aim is to learn about upcoming policies affecting their industries and develop relationships with people of influence, with a view to shaping policy that favours their interests.

Our study, published in the Sax Institute's peer-reviewed journal *Public Health Research and Practice*, systematically catalogues for the first time how widespread this practice is.

Out of sight

The movement of key people between government and tobacco industry roles without adequate transparency provides potential opportunities to influence policymaking out of sight. This can lead to delayed, weakened or suppressed implementation of tobacco control and anti-vaping reforms.

In Australia, tobacco industry interference tactics largely hinge on the industry's new product pipeline: e-cigarettes (vaping products). Examples of recent industry lobbying efforts to legalise the retail sale of nicotine vaping products include lobbying the federal government through submissions to legislative reviews, participating in inquiry hearings, making political donations, meeting privately with parliamentarians, funding third parties to lobby on their behalf, and sending unsolicited letters to ministers.

There is no suggestion any individual or organisation acted illegally, contravened employment guidelines or principles, or otherwise acted improperly – including in the performance of lobbying duties. However, the revolving door is important for tobacco companies as it provides opportunities to influence policymaking out of public sight.

Examples from overseas suggest the prospect of a lucrative future career in the private sector can be enough to influence decisions that favour industry while still in office. This can potentially undermine the quality and integrity of Australia's democratic system.

What can we do about it?

1. Greater public disclosure

There needs to be more extensive public disclosure of all tobacco company employees and lobbyists, either acting directly or via third-party allies. This information should be added to existing government registers, and also include detailed updates of activities and meetings.

2. Enforce 'cooling off' periods

We need to extend and enforce cooling-off periods – the minimum time required between switching from the public to the private sector. These range from twelve to eighteen months, depending on the role held in government. But our study showed these cooling-off periods are not being enforced, and there are no serious sanctions.

3. Update and enforce the law

Transparency and integrity legislation must be updated and enforced. Policies should be adopted in line with international best practices, such as those in Canada, to safeguard against the influence of tobacco companies in Australian policymaking.

4. Recognise the revolving door

We need to recognise revolving-door tactics as part of the implementation of the World Health Organization's Framework Convention on Tobacco Control. The Australian Government is a signatory to this convention. It has committed to protecting public health from the vested interests of the tobacco industry by publishing guidance for public officials on interacting with the tobacco industry. However, lobbying through the revolving door is not explicitly recognised or outlined in this guidance.

Here's why pharmacists are angry at script changes – and why the government is making them anyway

Henry Cutler
Macquarie University

Australians can now fill two months' supply of medicines at their community pharmacy, rather than one months', for 325 common medicines. This change, announced as part of the 2023–24 Budget, is expected to halve the cost of prescriptions for six million Australians.

But the Pharmacy Guild of Australia has taken exception to the government's policy change, warning it will create medicine shortages and make pharmacies financially worse off. The president of the guild wept at the thought of pharmacies going under because of reduced income from dispensing fees and co-payments.

Minister for Health and Aged Care Mark Butler was deft in his response, advising Australians to 'take advice around medicine supply and medicine shortages from our medicines authorities rather than the pharmacy lobby group'.

This argy-bargy between the government and the guild is not uncommon. What is uncommon is the public dismissal by a health minister of the guild's views. This government is using its political capital to push health reform forward and doesn't seem afraid to ruffle a few feathers.

What is the Pharmacy Guild of Australia?

The guild is an influential peak body registered under the federal *Fair Work Act 2009*. It acts like a union for community pharmacy (also known as chemist) owners. It provides resources to help pharmacists improve their small businesses, but most of its membership value comes from advocating for community pharmacy owners.

The Pharmaceutical Society of Australia is a separate group which represents all pharmacists, including those who work in hospitals and those who don't own the pharmacy they work in.

The guild and the society negotiate five-year agreements with the government on remuneration and funding for supplying Pharmaceutical Benefits Scheme (PBS) medicines in the community and for delivering pharmacy programs to support patients. The first of these, which are known as Community Pharmacy Agreements, was signed in 1990. The most recent (the seventh) was signed in 2020 and is due to expire in 2025, potentially having cost $25 billion over the five years. Of this, $16 billion will be paid for by the government and $9 billion will be paid for by patients.

How does the guild wield its power?

The guild is nearly 100 years old. It understands health care and how health policy is made. It has a reputation for shaping government health policy that is envied by many a healthcare peak body.

It doesn't have authority over government policy, but asserts its influence through its soft power by shaping community preferences to get patients behind what it wants. This stems from community pharmacies reaching every corner of Australia and the inherent trust between a pharmacist and a patient. The guild undertakes its own research to generate ideas and to criticise government policy when it suits.

The guild also takes a more direct approach to influencing government policy. The Australian Electoral Commission reported the guild was the thirteenth-largest political donor in 2021–22, donating $578,000 to political parties across eighty-eight separate donations. This was in an election year, which saw the doubling of the guild's donations compared to the previous year.

What policies has the guild influenced?

The extent of the guild's power is reflected in favourable policy outcomes for community pharmacies, despite these sometimes being unfavourable for taxpayers or patients.

The guild convinced the government to provide community pharmacies and pharmaceutical wholesalers with an extra $225 million in the 2017–18 Budget because prescription volumes were lower than expected within the sixth Community Pharmacy Agreement. This was a simple cash grab by pharmacies from taxpayers.

The guild also won a contentious policy backflip in 2018 by getting the government to retain the Pharmacy Location Rules, arguing they provide 'certainty and stability' for pharmacy small business.

What are the Pharmacy Location Rules?

The Pharmacy Location Rules are an agreement between the Australian Government and the Pharmacy Guild of Australia. They place restrictions on where a new pharmacy can be established or where an existing pharmacy can be relocated. Pharmacies must meet location-based criteria to be approved by the Australian Community Pharmacy Authority to receive pharmaceutical benefits.

The Pharmacy Location Rules do not allow new pharmacies to open within 1.5 kilometres or 10 kilometres of an existing pharmacy, depending on the location, distance to the nearest pharmacy, and the number of supermarkets and medical practitioners in the area. Unless an exemption applies, they do not allow pharmacies to be relocated from the town in which the approval was originally granted.

While no research has directly examined its impact, this policy has likely inflated consumer costs due to a restricted competitive pharmacy environment.

The Pharmacy Location Rules were introduced in the first Community Pharmacy Agreement to help larger pharmacies generate efficiencies and profit through scale. The rules sweetened accompanying restrictions on PBS remuneration from the government; these have been included in each subsequent Community Pharmacy Agreement.

The Pharmacy Location Rules were meant to expire in 2015 after a government-initiated Competition Policy Review recommended they 'should be removed in the long-term interests of consumers'. Instead, the guild pulled back on a threat to launch a major campaign against another government policy initiative, in exchange for delaying the removal of the location rules for five years.

Upon further lobbying, the Pharmacy Location Rules sunset clause was removed after the guild formed a Pharmacy Compact with the government in 2017.

Pharmacy policies that benefit consumers

Some government policy change has aligned guild and patient interests. Community pharmacists are increasingly providing services traditionally delivered by GPs. Pharmacists can now administer flu and COVID vaccines, and state trials allowing pharmacists to dispense oral contraception and antibiotics without a prescription are gaining favour.

This push towards greater scope of practice is embedded in the current and prior Community Pharmacy Agreements. But it threatens GP revenues.

The Australian Medical Association, the peak body for doctors, recently took a swing at the guild. It outlined ways to improve pharmacy competition in a government submission, which included removing Pharmacy Location Rules and getting pharmacies to compete on medicine prices through discounting.

What does this all mean for patients?

The government has assured the guild that the $1.2 billion savings from allowing patients to fill two months' supply of medicines will be invested directly back into pharmacies. The savings will be used to further expand the scope of practice for pharmacists, potentially informed by a National Scope of Practice Review.

Despite this assurance, the guild will fight. In addition to reduced dispensing fee revenue, having patients with chronic diseases cut back their pharmacy visits by half means the opportunity to sell other products sitting on shelves is also halved.

Substantial health reform is on the horizon, but it won't be painless. Policy change can upset embedded business models. It can impact livelihoods if providers don't respond to their new regulatory environment. In the coming whirlwind of power struggles, wouldn't it be nice if the government and providers worked together to put the patient first.

Our hometown, Mparntwe/Alice Springs, doesn't need more federal 'interventions'. A community-focused approach will work better

Chay Brown
Australian National University

Connie Shaw
Indigenous Knowledge

Kayla Glynn-Braun
Indigenous Knowledge

Shirleen Campbell
Indigenous Knowledge

Let us tell you about our town, our home. Mparntwe/Alice Springs is a small town on Arrernte Country in the red-hot heart of the land now called Australia. Our town, our home, is a place of beauty: spinifex-speckled, red sand dunes; black limestone after the rain; emerald waterholes nestled between the ranges; a wonderfully alive desert in one of the most remote places on Earth.

We hear more than 100 Indigenous languages being spoken on our streets every day, including Arrernte, Warlpiri, Luritja, Alyawarre and Pitjantjatjara. We are vibrant and multicultural. We are entrepreneurial. We love our sports, and our arts – and we cannot believe how much talent there is in our home.

But these are not the reasons our home was plastered across national media in early 2023. According to those news reports, a 'crime wave' or surge of 'alcohol-fuelled violence' was sweeping through our town. There was even talk of another military intervention.

Sensationalised media headlines and political pressure seem to be what prompted Prime Minister Anthony Albanese to make an impromptu trip to Alice Springs to meet with a handful of people, and introduce yet more alcohol restrictions. However, the media reports contained little to no context regarding the issues, and reinforced the same negative stereotypes that made the Northern Territory Emergency Response (or what we call 'the Intervention') possible.

What was the Intervention?

In 2007, in response to allegations of child sexual abuse in remote NT communities, the Australian Government suspended the *Racial*

Discrimination Act 1975 to make special laws for Aboriginal people in prescribed areas in the territory, and the military was rolled in.

The Intervention included a raft of measures such as compulsory income management in the form of the BasicsCard, imposing alcohol prohibitions on Aboriginal communities (although many of these communities already had self-determined dry policies), and mandatory health checks for Aboriginal children. Many of these measures remain in place today, including compulsory income management.

The Intervention caused long-term trauma and other harm for some First Nations people, and shame and negative racial stereotypes that still persist today. Shame and stigma compound violence, because they affect women's willingness to report or seek help.

Alcohol restrictions are not the answer

Alcohol policy in the Northern Territory has been driven by the harmful stereotype that all Aboriginal people are alcoholics. This is despite evidence non-Indigenous people in the Territory also consume disproportionately high amounts of alcohol. This is what the NT Government means when it says it wishes to move away from 'race-based policy'.

And while some Aboriginal Community Controlled Organisations support alcohol restrictions, many don't. Alcohol restrictions have never stopped drinking in the Northern Territory. Instead, they prompted onselling from within the Territory and from other locations, or more harmful forms of drinking involving mouthwash and hand sanitiser.

Alcohol and violence

Police and governments often claim alcohol leads to domestic violence–related assaults. However, administrative data, such as that captured by police, is very subjective and potentially unreliable.

The classification of 'alcohol-related assaults' and 'domestic violence–related assaults' is determined at the individual discretion of the attending police officer. In interviews we conducted for a new research project, some police officers stated they determined these classifications because they could smell alcohol, others because the person was slurring their words, and others because bottles of alcohol were present.

When questioned about whether the perpetrator or victim had to be drinking in order to make the classification of 'alcohol-related assault', the answer was invariably 'either' – meaning we do not know from police data whether the perpetrator was actually drinking alcohol. This begs the question: if the perpetrator is sober, should an assault against an intoxicated victim be included in alcohol-related statistics?

Alcohol alone does not cause domestic violence, although it can exacerbate it. As stated by Australia's national violence prevention organisation Our Watch, alcohol is often used as an excuse for domestic violence, rather than blaming the perpetrator. There are also reports of women being breathalysed when they present with injuries from domestic violence assaults to hospital. This means many may choose not to go, to avoid the shame and blame.

Despite domestic, family and sexual violence rates in the Northern Territory being the highest per capita in Australia, the Territory only receives a minuscule amount of funding compared with other states. In 2022, the Northern Territory received about $14 million in national partnership funding to address domestic, family and sexual violence. This was roughly 1.8 per cent of federal funding to address domestic or sexual violence.

And when shelters and specialist services such as Women's Safety Services of Central Australia and Tangentyere's Men's Behaviour Change Program are chronically underfunded, understaffed and under-resourced, this leaves very few resources for prevention or early intervention. Domestic, family and sexual violence intersect with – and exacerbate – other issues that already disproportionately affect the Northern Territory, such as overcrowding, homelessness, poor infrastructure, and lack of access to goods and services.

More police won't fix 'youth crime'

Last summer, there was an injection of thirty to forty extra police officers on the streets of Alice. This led to more arrests, but few outcomes.

Children who interact with police often end up in out-of-home care, removed from family and culture. Some end up in youth detention. Children who end up in youth detention are more likely to reoffend and go on to have further interactions with police and the judicial system.

The issue of young people, and sometimes very small children, roaming the streets late at night is distressing, and Alice Springs has been calling for a response to this for years. Many young ones travel in from the bush to stay in town to access services and visit family, and some get stuck here. And when unsupervised by adults, some young people do destructive things. Some of these children have grown up in overcrowding and poverty, and some are affected by foetal alcohol spectrum disorder.

In Alice Springs, there's basically nowhere kids can go to just bounce a ball with their mates that's accessible to everyone at any hour. Facilities are locked up, fenced off or out of reach financially for many children.

In 2021, the NT Government gave $4 million to the local council to develop a waterplay park in the town centre. But it took the money back while the council was struggling to decide on a site, and because it might attract more 'anti-social behaviour'.

Community support is needed, not punishments

Alice's problems stem from years of successive government and policy failure, chronic underfunding and under-resourcing. Harmful, reductive and racist media reporting has been detrimental to Alice and all who live here, particularly First Nations people.

We urge the federal and Territory governments to invest in our remote communities, and to fund and support a community-led response to the problems in Alice Springs. The response must be designed and led by local people. This must include the voices of young people, who have been unheard in all this noise.

Places such as Bourke, New South Wales have successfully addressed similar problems through justice reinvestment (redirecting money meant for prisons to the community), and this could inform local decision-making processes in Alice Springs, too.

Introducing a policy of needs-based funding would ensure the Northern Territory receives the funds it needs to begin to address domestic, family and sexual violence; overcrowding; support for those struggling with addiction; and programs to engage young people.

The media need to follow the guidelines in 'Media Changing the Story: Media Guidelines for the Reporting of Domestic, Family and Sexual Violence in the Northern Territory', which outlines how to engage with experts and communities, and report on violence in ways that are victim-survivor-centred, culturally safe and do no harm. Alice Springs can only be accurately reported through the voices of experts with experience of life here.

Alice's story is a story about geographic disadvantage. Alice needs community-led solutions, rather than punitive responses that bring shame, stigma and trauma. It's time we had the courage to do things differently.

Editor's note: Mandy Taylor from SNAICC – National Voice for our Children also contributed to this article.

Autism and ADHD assessment waits are up to two years' long. What can families do in the meantime?

Sarah Pillar
Telethon Kids Institute

Andrew Whitehouse
Telethon Kids Institute
University of Western Australia

Families in some parts of Australia are facing waitlists of up to two years to receive a diagnostic assessment for neurodevelopmental conditions such as autism and attention deficit hyperactivity disorder (ADHD). Assessment delays can create additional stress for families who are already worrying their child may be developing differently.

These waiting times are a symptom of the significant strain our health systems are under. System reform will take time and, in the meantime, there are many children who require urgent support. But supporting your child doesn't need to be put on hold while you wait for assessment.

Why are waitlists so long?

Diagnostic assessments are an important part of the clinical pathway for children developing differently. Diagnoses can provide parents and carers with a deeper understanding of their child. A diagnosis allows the child, their family and the supporting health professionals to benefit from all the information we have about that diagnosis, to understand how best to support the child going forward.

One reason why our diagnostic systems are currently under so much strain is expanding diagnostic boundaries. The criteria for autism and ADHD have changed over time, meaning more children now meet the criteria for these conditions than before.

Another reason is that our health, disability and education systems often require a formal diagnosis for a child to receive support. This further increases demand for diagnostic assessments.

Often, long waitlists result in children and families not getting timely access to crucial early-therapy services. Delays can mean that many of the best opportunities to support children's development early in life are missed, which can further entrench developmental disability and disadvantage.

However, importantly, there are many beneficial things that families can do in the meantime to pave the way for the future.

Three things families can do

While a diagnosis may help a child access support services, they are still able to access services without a diagnosis. If a parent is worried about their child's development, then it is important they continue to seek out support services while the child is on a diagnostic waitlist.

A GP is typically the best person to consult in the first instance. They can then refer the child and family to public or private therapy services. That said, private service options may involve out-of-pocket expenses, which can create inequity in access to services.

Parents can also take the following three steps.

1. Build connections with their child

A key part of all early supports is nurturing the connection parents have with their child. All children benefit from having frequent, meaningful time set aside to connect with their primary caregivers.

During this special connection time, parents might focus on slowing down, approaching their child with curiosity, being open to following their child's special interests, and trying a variety of strategies (including words, gestures or using pictures) to support communication.

Parents needn't feel pressure to spend all their time engaging with their child, but any time that can be dedicated to this will be time well spent.

2. Gather information to support diagnosis

Diagnoses of ADHD and autism are based on the observation of certain behaviours. A clinician will be able to observe some of these behaviours in their assessment, but they will also rely on information from parents about how their child usually behaves or interacts in different situations.

Parents can support this process by noting examples of the patterns of behaviours they've observed. These might include special interests, repetitive activities, social interactions, emotional regulation, sensory preferences or how their child communicates.

It is important parents don't only note what a child finds difficult, but also their strengths and interests. Sometimes, the things a child is particularly good at can tell us just as much as their challenges.

3. Prioritise family wellbeing

While parents are often proactive in seeking support for their child, they can sometimes neglect their own need for support. Parents are the most important people in a child's life, and parental capacity and wellbeing can have a significant influence on their child's outcomes.

While waiting for a diagnosis, parents should start to plan how they are also going to get the support they need. This can include staying connected within the community and making time for activities that bring them and their family joy.

Looking beyond diagnosis

When parents seek out a diagnosis for their child, they want help to support their child's development. But long waits for assessment and diagnosis can present barriers between Australia's health, education and disability systems and the help families need. The long waitlists to receive a diagnostic assessment are at odds with what we know about the importance of early intervention.

Recent clinical trials have shown how providing support to babies and parents at the first sign of developmental concern can lead to positive developmental outcomes for children. This approach prioritises acting quickly over diagnostic clarity, and makes it more likely children and families receive support during critical times in brain development.

As Australia seeks to reform its early childhood development system, the need of families to receive prompt support should be front of mind.

PART VII

Rethinking higher education

Editor's note: In 2023, the federal government called for ideas to reimagine higher education as part of a new Universities Accord between universities, governments, businesses and unions. The first four pieces in this section are part of our year-long series on experts' ideas for the accord.

Big ideas for how Australia funds and uses research

Brian Schmidt
Australian National University

Education makes Australian citizens healthier, wealthier and more engaged with society. At the same time, government-funded research in higher education drives economic productivity in ways other government funding does not. The future of Australian prosperity depends on both the education and research undertaken within its tertiary education system, and especially our universities.

The Australian higher education system has served the country well over the past thirty years, but it is not fit for the rapid pace of change to which the world will be subjected over the coming decades. If Australia is going to remain the 'Lucky Country', we are going to have to make more of our own luck.

The federal government's call for 'lasting reform' for Australian universities with the Universities Accord offers a timely opportunity to take action. In my personal submission to the accord process, I outline three big ideas to help reset higher education to deliver the system Australians need and deserve. The first is to provide each Australian with lifetime access to a single higher education system, spanning both university and vocational education.

In this piece, I want to focus on my other two big ideas: improving the way we fund and then translate research. These offer some of the biggest and easiest bang-for-buck solutions we can enact.

Australia's research ecosystem

Australia's research ecosystem has become highly reliant on funding via cross-subsidies from international student fees. Currently, Australian Government expenditure in research and development – expressed by the OECD as a fraction of GDP, termed 'government budget allocations for R&D' – is the lowest of the world's advanced economies and is continuing to decline. Instead, universities now spend more on research (using international student fees) than the government. This does not happen in other advanced economies.

Compounding this is the fact that government funding of directed research for national benefit is short-term, ad hoc, not strategically planned across agencies and poorly aligned to university planning timescales. Over the past seven years, as vice-chancellor of the ANU, I have seen dozens of different programs across various government agencies come and go with no overall coordination.

Research funding is also not fully integrated with workforce and major equipment needs, and this all leads to shortfalls in key areas of national research need. For example, if we look at critical minerals, the research infrastructure that underpins earth science is completely absent in planning and funding.

Universities, government and business are not working together on the big research issues facing Australia. To fix this, Australia urgently needs a fully funded, core, sovereign research capability. We also need to better translate research beyond universities to the real world.

We need to identify and properly fund sovereign research

Sovereign research capability is about Australia being able to fund and undertake the research it deems vital to its national interests. We must identify the core set of sovereign research capabilities necessary for the future security and prosperity of the Australian people. And we must fund these activities in full (including overheads), without the need for cross-subsidies from non-domestic sources. This requires a whole-of-government approach.

This core research should be expected to be uniformly excellent. It should include curiosity-driven research as well as research looking at practical solutions to existing problems ('applied research'). It should also go beyond technological developments to support the vibrancy of Australian democracy and culture.

A large fraction of the sovereign curiosity research money should be competitively allocated via existing bodies, including the Australian Research Council and National Health and Medical Research Council grant systems.

We need to make it easier to translate research

We must also rethink how we fund research translation for the public good. This is the process whereby we move research from labs or journals out into the real world.

When we fund applied research, we need to be strongly focused on outcomes. This includes the government directing funding for specific missions in areas of national need. This could be long-term, with time frames of five to twenty years.

Independent, expert-based boards would be given a budget to achieve specific goals within a time horizon, and invest across industry, government and the research sector to achieve these goals. This would replace current schemes for translating 'top-down' government priorities.

In addition, we need a new suite of agile 'bottom-up' supports for individuals' ideas. This would also replace existing research translation schemes, which have typically been 'set-and-forget' investments without expert stewardship over the ten-years-plus cycle necessary to get globally competitive capability.

Projects should be closely monitored and defunded when progress is deemed insufficient. Expert panels could also work with the private sector to rapidly increase investment in such programs when commercially justified.

Funding programs need to pay particular attention to the areas of market failure. Such a system should not crowd out existing private technology transfer but do things that will not otherwise happen, and better connect industry, government and academia in the research ecosystem.

Blue-sky thinking

The foundational research done in universities underpins the sovereign capability of the nation to increase productivity, improve health and wellbeing, remain secure, and solve and adapt to challenges that face society. This is the research universities do that leads to new products, jobs and industries never envisaged when the research cycle begins.

Work just in my own area of astro-particle physics has underpinned the wi-fi, camera, Global Positioning System and touchscreen aspects of your phone, not to mention many recent startups across Australia.

But most of the value created for Australia is actually through indirect productivity spillovers. These are the people, ideas and capabilities created by Australian research that find their way in thousands of ways into Australian society, and which allow us to do more for less. These are hard to measure, and emerge with a considerable lag, but our best estimates are that they are large. Government has a special role in funding this activity, as firms cannot typically capture the benefits of this work.

International education is becoming increasingly globally competitive. The margin from international student fees that Australian universities are so reliant on to fund their research is bound to drop over coming decades. So, as part of a sovereign research capacity, Australia should set a minimum level for government-sponsored foundational research as a fraction of GDP. This would bring Australia in line with other nations with advanced economies.

And if all universities are expected to undertake excellent research, a base amount of research funding should be made available either through student-based allocations or another mechanism. Alternatively, new types of future higher education institutions could have research dropped from their missions entirely.

Making our own luck

Australian universities and their research have for many years made Australians' lives and our world better. The government's accord process gives us the chance to make sure our universities can continue to deliver on this promise for our future generations.

But we must act, and this action must take serious stock of how we fund and translate research in Australia today. If we fail to value and fund university research in the way that we need, and should, the so-called Lucky Country might just run out of luck.

Australia has way more PhD graduates than academic jobs. Here's how to rethink doctoral degrees

Sam Hoang
Victoria University

Binh Ta
Monash University

Hang Khong
Monash University

Trang Thi Doan Dang
Monash University

One of the key reasons for doing a doctoral research degree or PhD is to pursue an academic career. But this dream is becoming increasingly far-fetched, due to a decline in academic positions and a steady increase in Australians undertaking PhDs.

The number of PhD completions has been steadily growing over the past two decades, from about 4000 to about 10,000 per year. According to our calculations, based on the information available, the cumulative number of people in Australia with a PhD increased from about 135,000 in 2016 to about 185,000 in 2021.

But the number of academic positions has shrunk. Australia saw a significant decrease in academic staff, from 54,086 in 2016 to 46,971 in 2021, as universities cut costs during the pandemic. These figures have been adjusted for life expectancy and overseas PhD graduates returning to their home country.

With the Universities Accord review examining how our higher education system needs to work, we need to rethink who is doing a PhD and how their degrees are structured.

Where do PhDs want to work?

There are plenty of incentives to keep PhD candidates coming through the system. Some federal government funding to universities is based on research degree completions. PhDs are also free for domestic students. On top of this, universities put pressure on academic staff to supervise successful PhD students – this is used as one of the criteria for promotions.

There is no official data on how many PhD graduates go on to work in academia. About 25 per cent of PhD graduates got some employment in academia, according to a small-scale survey in 2011. Our estimates suggest this figure has not changed much as of 2021. If there are about 185,000 people with a PhD, this is four times higher than the number of available academic positions (46,971).

We also know some PhD students struggle to get work outside of academia, despite the prestigious nature of their qualifications. The 2022 Graduate Outcomes Survey found 84.7 per cent of research degree graduates (which includes masters degrees by research as well as PhDs) were in full-time employment within six months of completing their studies. This compares with 78.5 per cent of undergraduates.

Not all PhD candidates and graduates want an academic career, however. A 2019 national survey found 51 per cent of all PhD students wanted to find a job in business or the public sector. But here, students' field of study makes a big difference.

Two-thirds of PhD students in STEM fields (science, technology, engineering and maths) were hoping to work in industry. The banking, civil engineering, mining, energy and medical/pharmaceutical sectors are the top employers of PhD graduates.

Meanwhile, two-thirds of PhD students in social sciences, including history, politics, education, sociology, psychology, economics and anthropology, wanted to stay in academia.

Our study

To understand how people with social sciences PhDs navigate employment, we conducted twenty-three in-depth interviews with doctoral graduates from five Australian universities – all interviewees graduated less than five years before the interviews. Our research uncovered two distinct themes.

First, a stable academic job is almost impossible to find. Of the group, only one had gained a continuing academic position within five years of graduation. Thirteen were on precarious contracts (either casual or fixed-term), while three were doing a 'postdoc' or research fellowship (which also often involve a fixed-term contract). Six worked in either the private sector or government.

As one interviewee told us, PhD candidates should

> put aside the assumption that … because you've got a PhD, you will automatically get a job. That's not the case. There are many many many PhDs out there who cannot find work or are working in what we call menial jobs or 'survivor' jobs.

Another emphasised the insecure nature of working in academia:

> I've been working as a sessional [employed on contracts per semester] in higher education, basically full-time on a million contracts.

Some participants moved in and out of academia while holding slim hope of finding a continuing position:

> If I don't get an academic job within one year or two years, then it's kind of over for me.

The second theme we identified was a lack of career support or preparation for graduates. While ongoing academic jobs were very difficult to obtain, PhD graduates said they were not well prepared for the labour market outside academia.

There is a sharp contrast between university and non-university occupations in terms of workplace cultures and employer expectations. For example, industry employers want skills needed for work rather than qualifications or publications. PhD graduates moving out of academia have had to retrain themselves.

As one participant told us:

> They were less impressed by the publications. They were more interested in the skills that I got … So I did some online data courses [like] LinkedIn courses, and then I tried to apply for some jobs with these skills and in this direction.

Another participant said they had to hide their doctoral degree for fear of being seen as overqualified. Meanwhile, meaningful career advice was thin on the ground.

> [My university] didn't actually do anything to support me in getting my job.

How to rethink doctoral education

The diverse and insecure employment outcomes of the PhD graduates in our study strongly point to a need for universities to rethink how they educate PhD students.

First, this includes offering specific career education as part of PhD programs. This may require universities to be up-front about the employment prospects for PhD graduates and the research funding climate.

Career consultations from both universities' career centres and industry experts should be offered early in PhD programs to help students make informed decisions about future options. For those who would like to pursue a traditional academic career, it is important to have ongoing career guidance from their supervisors and research offices.

Second, there needs to be more structured work experience. Universities should strengthen their partnerships with industry to facilitate work experience. Those seeking academic jobs also need to be provided with meaningful opportunities to work alongside academic staff in both teaching activities and research projects.

Third, universities need to ensure doctoral programs better prepare students for employment possibilities inside and outside academia. This includes opportunities to build transferable skills such as teamwork, communication, analytical skills and leadership. This specifically needs to include teaching students how to write and speak for different audiences beyond academia, including policymakers and the public.

This needs to include admissions

Lastly, we also need to take a hard look at PhD admissions. There is currently no limit on PhD numbers, and the more admissions universities have, the more funding they will earn when students graduate. To balance supply and demand, the government should consider quotas for funding PhD students in each field. This would also help select the most suitable PhD candidates, those who will most likely benefit from the rigours of doctoral study.

This may not be a popular move, but we have to be more realistic about whether accepting more and more people into three-plus years of intense study is benefiting the students or simply generating funds for universities.

Why arts degrees and other generalist programs are the future of Australian higher education

Catharine Coleborne
University of Newcastle

There is a persistent idea that a generalist degree, such as a Bachelor of Arts, is less likely to land you a job when compared with a specific qualification. This is personified by the stereotypical arts student as a directionless young person who has chosen to explore sprawling and eclectic subjects with no clear outcomes.

This was reinforced by the introduction of the Job-ready Graduates Package in 2020, which made most arts and humanities subjects more expensive to study from 2021. The cost of a Bachelor of Arts degree rose by 113 per cent. Universities Australia has since called for Job-ready Graduates to be scrapped, noting that 'price signals as a driver of student choice simply do not work'.

Either way, the idea that a generalist degree just leads to overqualified graduates serving coffee *Reality Bites*–style is not only wrong, it is also a misguided understanding of what we need from graduates today and in the future.

Arts degrees do lead to jobs

Research shows social sciences and humanities graduates are getting jobs after their studies.

The 2022 Graduate Outcomes Survey found almost 73 per cent of humanities, culture and social sciences graduates were working in a range of government, non-government and business roles within several months of graduating. This was an increase of 15 per cent on the previous year, and was noticeably better than the overall average increase of just under 10 per cent.

Why are we so fixated on 'vocations'?

Since the 19th century, 'work' has been understood through types of 'occupations' that were undertaken for a significant period of a person's life, with opportunities for improvement and promotion, and potentially framed as 'careers'. But the idea that individuals train to learn a set of skills or knowledge that prepares them for one stable career is outdated.

What US professor Frank Parsons (considered the father of careers counselling) called 'choosing a vocation' in 1909 has been supplanted by employers who want people who are good at problem-solving and analytical thinking, have digital skills, and can demonstrate leadership, initiative and resilience. We also need to reposition our understanding of 'employability' by considering the uncertain future that university graduates are heading into.

Along with the threat of further pandemics and climate change, we face increased global conflict and important questions about how to support displaced peoples in our own region and around the world. There is also growing anxiety about what AI will mean for our lives and workplaces.

Research shows our society will need the skills, deep knowledge and understanding to reframe what it means to create cohesive multicultural and diverse communities. It will need to support all lives – including the very young and the aged – with meaning and purpose in order to forge humanity's future. To do this, we should reimagine the future workforce through values, competencies and skills, not 'professions'.

The rapid social change we are undergoing means future graduates will need to be highly flexible. Vocational degree training as we have understood it could leave students stranded, lacking the critical capability to understand how to adapt to new roles. For example, leaders in the profession of social work have predicted the vocational degree may need to be replaced by agile skills.

This is where the generalist degree comes in

This is why the generalist degree has a big part to play in the emerging higher education landscape for graduates. Humanities, social sciences, general science, technology and creative industries fields such as design can deliver adaptable, flexible mindsets.

Generalist graduates learn to argue, debate, discuss, engage with ideas, write and present. These degrees also offer so-called 'soft skills' such as emotional intelligence, communication and teamwork.

What if the upcoming Universities Accord decided that generalist degrees, not vocational qualifications, were the future of university learning in Australia? This could see the creation of more public–private partnerships to increase work experience and practical opportunities during study. This could in turn create experiences in the community, industry and government.

In doing this, we should embrace the possibility of the broad curriculum that is offered by arts, humanities, social sciences and general science degrees, but insist on elevating their transferable skills to set students up for a lifetime of work and learning. However, a shift towards revaluing – and even elevating – generalist degrees will require a radical unpacking of degree structures, ways of teaching and learning, fee structures and models.

More students in Australia could be encouraged to expand their learning in a wide range of areas, but specialise and choose pathways by their second or third year of study, with postgraduate credentials to follow.

Valuing young peoples' choices

Recent history tells us human adaptability will help us face future threats. Young people want to engage in learning that will prepare them for futures we don't yet see. Valuing the generalist degree – with graduates able to enjoy learning, to develop the courage to think, reflect, interpret, evaluate, humanise, respond and create – will give young people confidence and a sense of their own agency.

Such a model could be world-leading.

DIY degree? Why universities should make online educational materials free for all

Richard F Heller
University of Newcastle

As part of the federal government's bid to overhaul higher education, the Universities Accord discussion paper is seeking to 'widen' opportunities for people to access university. It also wants to 'grow a culture' of lifelong learning in Australia. As the review team notes, most people in Australia who study at university are under thirty-five.

Lifelong learning can help ensure workforce skills are up to date and jobs in high demand can be filled, as well as enabling people to create new job opportunities through innovation. These issues need to be approached in many ways, and they will inevitably include proposals for shorter forms of learning as well as addressing the financial cost of attending university.

My proposal is that a proportion of educational resources generated by publicly funded universities should be made public and freely available. This could radically expand opportunities and flexibility, and potentially allow students to design their own degrees by doing multiple different units from different universities.

This idea is not completely new

There is a precedence for this idea. The international Plan S initiative is led by a group of national research funding organisations. Since 2018, it has been pushing for publicly funded research to be published in open-access journals or platforms. Australian chief scientist Cathy Foley similarly wants all Australian research to be 'open access, domestically and internationally, and for research conducted overseas to be freely available to read in Australia'.

When it comes to university learning, a 2019 UNESCO report encouraged member states to make higher education educational resources developed with public funds free and freely available. Meanwhile, in a March 2023 report, the Productivity Commission recommended the federal government require 'all universities to provide all lectures online and for free'. The commission said this would increase transparency in teaching performance and encourage online learning. But this also has the ability to make higher education more accessible.

There is already plenty of international experience sharing educational materials online, including the global Open Educational Resources public digital library. This includes resources from early learning through to adult education.

The Productivity Commission says universities would not lose income by making educational resources open-access. This is because universities 'sell' credentials, not resources. It is also argued overworked academics can save time by using materials created by others.

But there is resistance from institutions and academics, including a perception free resources will be of poor quality and take a lot of time to create. There is also a lack of technological tools with which to adapt resources. This may explain why open education has not yet taken off in Australia.

How would this work?

My plan would require open online sites to host educational materials produced by academics. These would need to be moderated or curated and published under an open-access licence.

It would include a peer review system for educational materials like the one already used for research publications. Academics could get credit for publishing, updating or reviewing resources, and the publication of education output would be included in university metrics.

This could also help reverse the current downgrading of teaching in Australian universities in favour of research.

There could be three types of users:

- students who access materials through the university that produced them, as per current practice
- individual students outside the university who access materials for their own learning at whatever stage of life

- other organisations, including other universities, that then contextualise and deliver the materials to their students.

What kinds of materials are we talking about?

The Productivity Commission has talked about 'lectures' being made available for free. But lectures are not a good way of transmitting information, especially online. For one thing, they do not promote critical thinking.

My plan proposes that whole courses, or at least sections of courses with assessments, would be provided. This includes text, videos and software, as well as potentially course-planning materials and evaluation tools. An indication of the academic level to which the course speaks, and the amount of possible credit, should also be provided.

What about accreditation?

Accreditation of learning should be considered as part of this.

The OERu is an international organisation where partner universities – including the University of Southern Queensland and Curtin University in Australia, and Otago Polytechnic and Ako Aotearoa in New Zealand – offer free access to online courses. Students pay reduced fees if they want to submit assignments, which can earn them microcredits towards a degree offered by one of the partners.

A more radical option would be to develop a system where students collect microcredits from whatever source they wish and present them to an accrediting body for an academic award, rather than enrolling in a particular degree course.

Suggested recommendations

The Universities Accord review team should recommend three things:

1. Most university-generated educational material should be public and free.
2. As an interim goal, within three years, 10 per cent of all public university courses should be freely available online.
3. An organisation should be created to develop the infrastructure needed to do this. This includes open repositories, a peer-review system for open educational materials, and systems for offering microcredits to students and academic credit to academics who take part.

The Productivity Commission says making this material public will encourage higher-quality teaching, empower students and assist in lifelong learning. On top of this, there is the potential for true reform of the educational landscape.

It provides opportunities for collaboration between universities, rather than a competitive business model. And it would make teaching more important, rather than an 'inconvenient task' to be performed by those seeking academic advancement through research.

Finally, it would genuinely make learning more accessible and more affordable, no matter who you are or where you live.

'Battered and broken. I must get out': What staff told us about teaching and working in New Zealand universities today

Nik Taylor
University of Canterbury
Zoei Sutton
Flinders University

The current funding crisis in NZ universities has not happened in a vacuum. It is a by-product of the neoliberal 'reforms' introduced here in the 1980s and which have affected every aspect of university work.

Nor is this confined to New Zealand. The stress on corporate capitalism, adoption of business practices and prioritisation of economic goals over all others have transformed higher education in the Western world.

We see this time and again when universities cite financial losses and implement staff cuts. This has many consequences, including the exploitation of unpaid labour by casual staff. Submissions to the Australian Senate Select Committee on Job Security suggested underpayment of casual teaching staff in Australian universities is rampant.

The same applies in New Zealand, but the problem is likely worse than we know. Workers whose employment is precarious are unlikely to complain about their working conditions for fear of compromising future employment prospects.

Full-time staff are struggling, too. Intensification of workloads, job insecurity amid seemingly constant restructures, pressures to obtain competitive external funding, research excellence and student outcome targets, and toxic work environments are all threats to staff wellbeing.

To understand how university workers experience these realities of the modern university, our current project aims to capture their voices and stories. And those stories make for a depressing read.

'Constantly drowning'

To build empathy and understanding between workers with different experiences – precarious and permanent, faculty and professional staff, workers with disability and so on – we shared their anonymised posts on our open online site, Working in the Modern University. In their stories, we hear about how the intensification of casual workloads leads to forced choices between poor-quality teaching or working unpaid hours. We hear how staff feel trapped in a cycle of exhaustion, futility, guilt and hopelessness.

Some describe how precarious life has become, either in or on the edge of poverty, constantly managing insecurity for little financial or personal reward. And we hear of people feeling 'battered and broken', of 'constantly drowning', and of feeling complicit in creating a 'caricature of education'.

Reading these stories is hard. They speak of increased desperation, grief for a system that could be so much more, and a loss of hope from staff who also see this reflected in their students.

Without rapid and real change, we fear a future where the university's role of nurturing critical thinkers is vastly diminished, and where research on and with marginalised people and ideas is replaced by sanitised research linked to economic priorities. That would mean the closure of one of the few places left where 'noisy conversations' about democracy and political alternatives can take place.

The public good

The shift to seeing students as customers or clients – on the pathway to becoming 'job-ready graduates' – has also moved the focus away from developing critical thinking skills and towards vocational training, pastoral care and keeping clients happy. One contributor wrote of:

> the reinvention of the university as a place to train people for a capitalist workforce instead of developing their intellectual and creative potential more holistically.

This is unfortunate for students, who pay dearly for their education but receive a 'less than inspiring educational experience'. As another contributor wrote:

> Students expect to study full-time and achieve good grades while working full-time because the neoliberal complex implies this is possible. Meanwhile, student-to-teaching-staff ratios grow amidst bulging workloads and ... student feedback on our performance can make or break us.

Knowledge is affected, too. Staff are often on the receiving end of student complaints when topic material is complex or grades don't match expectations. This deters teaching that challenges students, develops critical thinking or requires student engagement.

Similarly, research priorities have shifted. Universities no longer prioritise academics using their expertise to innovate and investigate for the public good. Instead, they are pressured to pursue externally funded research, tailored to suit the appetite of a government or prevailing public opinion.

We have also seen a rise of the 'subcontract model', where 'lead' researchers no longer create the research products they 'sell', but rely on casual and fixed-term research assistants who are often under-acknowledged.

Funding for critical thinking

We need to see a return to the idea of funding education as a public good in and of itself (granted, a radical idea under neoliberalism). Alongside this, we need to separate education from current culture wars and recognise the value of arts, humanities and social sciences.

It's no accident that the focus of frequent cuts by corporate-minded universities is on disciplines that teach critical-thinking skills. While this may be partly due to declining student numbers, there's certainly a case to be made that it reflects government priorities and rhetoric around 'instrumentalised' education.

And we need proper funding for research that isn't tied to government policy or ideology.

Academics are not short of ideas about the future of higher education, from the practical to the idealistic. The proliferation of books, papers and conferences on the subject attests to this. Universities would do well to heed their own experts on this critical issue.

PART VIII

Searching for identity and belonging

'I have been trained to be an engineer ... now, I am a pickle seller!' What does migration do to a wife?

Farjana Mahbuba
Australian Catholic University

'But you know what's funny? All my life, I have been trained to be an engineer. Look at me now, I am a pickle seller!'

She laughed with teary eyes. I did not laugh. I felt like crying and giving her a tight hug. Yet I did not move. I kept listening. I am a researcher. I am supposed to just collect data. I am not supposed to respond emotionally.

By the way, how does one collect data when the 'subjects' are human? When the information one is looking for has turned into personal stories? Like this story of Selina (a pseudonym), born in a riverside town near Dhaka, the capital of Bangladesh. Selina's husband was already planning to apply for an Australian offshore visa when they married and in 2010, when she was twenty-seven, the couple migrated to Sydney.

On the occasion of her birth, Selina's grandmother had held her closely to her chest, telling her mother: 'Beti [dear daughter], in our family, girls are strong. Make her strong. I may not live long to see her grow, but promise me, you'll make her strong.'

Her mother kept the promise. She made Selina an engineer.

To my Australian readers, a girl being an engineer may not mean much. Only my Bangladeshi readers will know a girl being an engineer means her parents were constantly bombarded with wellwishers' remarks: 'Why are you wasting your money on making your girl an engineer? What's in it for you? She will be married to someone and go off to her in-laws!'

She was made the centre of jokes by her friends: 'Hey, here comes our engineer! Once married, her engineering skills will make her cooking more delicious!'

She was ridiculed by her teachers whenever she stumbled on something difficult that she couldn't understand at one go: 'Why are you wasting your time in this engineering class? Better you do cooking classes in the kitchen!'

A Bangladeshi girl, an engineer: it means she and her parents fought all the way for her to complete the degree and enter the profession.

So, when she said, 'Look at me now,' I literally looked at her. Looked at her teary eyes. Looked at her clean, tidy, beautifully organised house.

Looked at her, cooking and talking to me simultaneously – her kids would be back from school soon – having just moved the pickle jars from the shade to the sunny places on the kitchen verandah, so a carpenter could fix the broken deck in the backyard.

There was a time when Selina was busy with her daily hectic routine as a civil engineer working in Bangladesh. She enjoyed those days very much. She felt proud going to work. Just like the other women in her family, who are either doctors or engineers, she had made a name for herself.

Overeducated, underemployed

No, no-one forced Selina to leave her profession when she moved to Australia. At the same time, no-one guided her or told her how to rebuild her career in this foreign land.

Selina's case is not unique. Bangladeshis are a relatively new migrant community. Mostly they arrived in Australia through overseas scholarship programs during the late 1970s and the early 1980s, and later, from 2006 to 2011, through the general skilled migration program.

According to 2021 census data, 51,491 people in Australia were born in Bangladesh. Bangladeshi Muslim women here have significantly higher educational attainment than the wider Australian female population. The data shows 19.71 per cent of Bangladeshi Muslim women in Australia have a postgraduate degree, compared with 7.95 per cent of women in general. Overall, 22.75 per cent of Bangladeshi Muslim women have a bachelor's degree, compared with 15.87 per cent of women across the board.

The same census data shows the unemployment rate to be 5.31 per cent among Bangladeshi Muslim women, compared to 2.21 per cent in the wider female population. Salma Bint Shafiq, in her research into Bangladeshi migrants in Australia, has found non-participation in the labour market is much more common for these women (30 per cent) than it is for men (2 per cent).

'When I came to Australia,' said Selina, 'I knew no-one except my husband.' He is from a totally different profession and was struggling to make an entrance. Selina was aware of her ticking biological clock and did not want to miss out on motherhood. She'd already delayed motherhood because of the prospect of migration. And she had one of those pregnancy experiences where you constantly throw up. You can't hold even a sip of water down. She had to carry a poly bag in her hand at all times because she would vomit without any warning, anytime, anywhere.

After the pregnancy, there was simply no time. Her husband was working a second job to support his own study, career and family. She was there, alone, to recover from the baby blues, and at the same time take care of a difficult baby who didn't want to sleep at night. Two separate specialists gave the same verdict: some babies are just like that.

It's interesting how one single step backward in one's career starts an avalanche of falling behind. Eventually, there was a second baby, and there were some attempts in between to study something related to the engineering field.

Oh, I just said it in a single sentence, didn't I?

In reality, it didn't happen that easily. There was extreme physical exhaustion, blood and sweat, month after month of sleepless nights, so much confusion with new babies, isolation, living like a single mum with two young kids all alone while the father was struggling to rebuild a career and doing two jobs. Which is not uncommon. Recent ABS statistics show 57 per cent of skilled visa holders have had two or more jobs simultaneously since arrival.

'Losing myself bit by bit'

What does a new country do to a migrant wife? I met Selina to listen to her financial experiences, to identify any pattern of financial abuse in her spousal relationship. I ended up discovering how she went from engineer to pickle seller.

So far in my fieldwork, collecting 'data' on spousal financial abuse, I have spoken to more than a dozen Bangladeshi migrant Muslim women living in New South Wales. In our in-depth interviews, stories similar to Selina's have started to emerge. I met Jasmin and Shimul (both pseudonyms), one a former banker and the other a university lecturer before she migrated. Both were unable to resume their careers here. Said Jasmin, 'The moment I stepped out of the airport, everything was new to me. Even the sky looked different. I have never seen such a blue sky in my life. The people looked different. All my life I was a very good student in English, but I could not understand a single word they were talking. Instead of feeling joy and excitement, [it was] as if I was losing myself bit by bit into the unknown. It was traumatic.'

Both Jasmin and Shimul became pregnant shortly after arrival, giving birth for the first time, alone in a new land, without a single family member being around. Often, their husbands are busy with second jobs to earn extra money to support the family.

I see a pattern emerging. A pattern where a migrant woman's financial misery starts on day one of her journey to Australia. The day she steps into an unknown world, where her only bridge to this world is her husband. A husband who himself is often extremely busy earning enough money to support his two families – the new family in Australia, and his own parents and siblings back home in Bangladesh.

Intentionally or not, the wife is left alone, isolated and uninformed. She gets lost. And the impact lasts for many years to come. Financially and otherwise, she gradually becomes totally dependent on her husband.

For some couples, it does not take long for the husband to turn his wife's financial dependency into a tool to control her mobility. Spousal financial abuse thrives when one partner starts manipulating, deceiving or coercing to create or maintain the other partner's dependency.

'Do they think I am a robot?'

'Do you want to try some?' Selina offered me three different types of pickles on a plate. I accepted. Not doing so would have been rude. The pickles were delicious, made of mango, olive and mixed fruits.

'How come you make such delicious pickles? Did you learn to make pickles before you came here?'

She started laughing at my question. This time not with tears. My question was so funny to her that she held her stomach to balance her body's vibration. Her laughter was contagious. Through my laughter, I managed to ask, 'What's so funny about this question?'

'It's that …' She was still trying to get a hold of her laughter. 'It's just that I have never made pickle in my life before! … My mother never asked me to cook or to do any house chores because I was busy with my study. I was pampered in my house. Everyone knew studying engineering isn't easy.'

'How come you make pickles now?'

Her laughter slowly wore off. One day she looked at her two young kids. She looked at the social media profiles of colleagues she once worked with in Bangladesh, now being promoted to senior positions. 'You know how it feels?' she asked me. 'It feels like as if that was another life when I was an engineer. As if that life was a dream. These past many years, I was so busy making a home in this foreign land, going through difficult pregnancies, giving birth twice, and looking after these two kids who just started to go to school recently, coming so far almost all alone, somehow along the way, I have become someone else.'

A silence fell upon us. She turned her back to me, cleaning some dishes in the kitchen basin. Or did she just try to hide her tears?

She said, 'Everyone is so proud of my husband now that he is doing well in his field. At the same time, I can clearly see the pity in their eyes for me. No-one says anything, they don't need to. People can say so much without actually saying it out loud. After my second kid started school last year, I heard this a lot: "Now you can go back to your career, can't you?" I just smile. Do they think I am a robot? Just switch off the career one day, and after many years of having your life upside down, switch it back on and go restart the career? No-one talks about the years of the [employment] gap that put me at the bottom of the list or maybe out of the list. No-one talks about how lost I feel now. The first few weeks when my second kid went back to school, I felt so lost, I walked on the road alone for hours, didn't know where I was going.'

The silence again. So heavy on me I felt uncomfortable. I tried to concentrate on the pickles on the plate. I put the rest in my mouth. Would she tell me how she became a pickle seller? I did not want to ask the question again.

She turned towards me, a strange smile on her face. She said: 'One day, I felt so pathetic that I wanted to do something totally different … So, I tried to make pickles from a YouTube recipe. That's the first time in my life I made pickles. My husband usually does not like pickles. But when he tried my pickles, he was surprised at how tasty it was. He jokingly said, "You know, people will actually buy this!" I suddenly thought, why not try to make pickles and sell them? Something that I can do from the house while not disturbing my set-up routine of taking care of house chores, looking after kids' studies, dropping them off and picking them up from school … So, I did. I opened up a Facebook page and started to sell pickles. And it worked!'

She looked at my plate and said, 'Oh! You finished them! How lovely. Would you like more?'

No, I did not want more, though they were really delicious. Her story was enough to fill me up.

That choice

Do I see myself a little bit in her story? What about my own struggle as a Bangladeshi migrant woman in this foreign land? Was that not me who went from shop to shop in malls with copies of a handwritten CV to drop off, looking for any kind of job, any kind of job at all?

Was that not me who one day burst into a flood of tears, crying to another Bangladeshi woman, 'What's the use of me being the best student in my class? I understand not a single word they say! What kind of English is this?!'

Was that not me who one night, when coming home after a long shift working at a chain shop, was the subject of a racial slur by a drunk white man? The man was shouting F-words in front of a platform full of people waiting for the same train. Not a single person asked him to stop shouting.

And was that not me who had decided to leave her profession after her second child was born, who herself had to make that impossible choice, a choice between an academic career and motherhood? How many of us can really manage to bounce back after a sharp fall like that? It took five years of struggle for me to come back to academia, but that's another story for another time.

After a long interview, I said goodbye to Selina. I was walking back to my car when I thought, how many migrant women are out there with similar kinds of stories? They come to this country with such high hopes and dreams.

Since I started doing this fieldwork, whenever I see a visibly recognisable migrant woman, walking down the road, in the supermarket or in the playground with kids, I wonder: what's her story? What kind of dream did she have when she first came to Australia? Did Australia help her realise her dreams, or did it become the graveyard of her dreams?

I wonder.

Brenda Matthews was ripped from a loving family twice. But she was born too late to be officially recognised as part of the Stolen Generations

Sandra Phillips
Western Sydney University

The woman's face is in profile, her eyes looking into the distance – or the past, or the future. This is a quiet woman, a thoughtful one; possibly one who also carries sadness in her soul. This woman's face is natural, a face with features as familiar as my own – a strong brow, deep-set and dark eyes, and full unvarnished lips set with an appealing cupid's bow. Her hair is swept up, the background is purple-blue – evocative of a beautiful night sky.

I don't know why it takes me the full read of her book before I see the photograph of two children superimposed on her right cheek: one child white-skinned with blonde hair, the other dark-skinned with dark hair. It's a happy photo, as natural as they come. Before this photograph of the children came into focus, my mind's eye assumed it was white ochre, placed ready for a ceremony of some sort.

The book, *The Last Daughter*, recounts the woman's life to a certain midlife point. It ends with insight into the making of a documentary feature film, released in June 2023. The book is a ceremony of sorts: a bringing together of the woman's story of families, Country, love, separation, heartache. And at its centre, a truth-seeking quest to right the wrongs perpetrated by a government hell-bent on doing 'as they saw fit' when it came to Aboriginal people, with little regard for the consequences.

The author is Brenda Matthews nee Simon, born 1970. This birth year renders her officially ineligible for being recognised as part of the stolen generations. The *New South Wales Aborigines Protection Act* was repealed and the Aboriginal Welfare Board abolished in 1969. She was removed from her family four years later, in 1973.

Stolen, again and again

Brenda was one of eight children, seven of whom were heartbreakingly removed from and then haphazardly returned to their parents, Brenda Simon nee Hammond and Gary Simon. Brenda was the last to be returned home – after five years. She was two years old when she was taken and seven when she was returned.

She describes her mother's memory of doing the household chores with a friend one day, 'a few days' after she took her sick child Karla to the local hospital. 'A car pulled up outside and two Welfare Department officers got out,' writes Brenda. Her friend asked if they'd come to inspect the house. 'Welfare officers were often inspecting Aboriginal homes to check if they were clean, which was often an excuse and a precursor to taking the children.'

But they had arrived 'to take the kids', on mysterious charges of neglect. Local knowledge about collusion between the local hospital matron and the Welfare Department does not escape mention.

After three months in a home, Brenda was fostered by a white family, who had a daughter of a similar age. 'She is my younger sister and I love her,' recalls Brenda in the book. They believed they had adopted Brenda, and that a single mother had given her up. Five years later she was returned home, with almost no transition. 'I was ripped from both these families,' she writes, looking back.

This memoir reveals Brenda reconciling with this past, forty years later, bringing her 'Black family' and her 'White family' together. The trauma impacts of these separations can be read through this life story, not least

Brenda Matthews with her children
Source: Provided by the author.

when eighteen-year-old Brenda tells no-one she is pregnant and ends up giving birth alone in her bedroom:

> I think deep down inside, I'm scared of this baby being taken from me because I was taken away from my Mum and Dad. I don't want history to repeat itself.

Baby Keisha enjoys unbroken bonds with her parents and both extended families. Later, she is joined by four brothers, then by four more siblings, through her mother's marriage to stepfather Mark. By the end of this book, Keisha has two children of her own, who become central to Brenda's commitment to her story, her families and a future free from cruel intervention.

History as told in *The Last Daughter* – family separation and its resulting trauma – does not repeat for future generations. But its effects continue to find sad reverberation in the life experiences of Brenda, her parents and her siblings.

Before her own children were 'shoved' into a government car, Brenda's mum had lived in fear of exactly this – as a teenager, she'd witnessed a cousin taken from her Aunty Greta. Thinking about these removals under

Brenda with her 'White sister', Rebecca
Source: Provided by the author.

false charges, Brenda wonders what other lies are recorded as fact in government files about other family members, particularly after uncovering – with the help of historian and Wiradjuri woman Kim Burke – that Brenda's maternal grandmother and great-grandmother were also stolen.

> What chance did we have? Stolen, again and again and again. This is one family heirloom that didn't need passing down, and the only blessing is that Mum was not stolen.

'This is real history'

Members of Brenda's white family are also left affected by the brutality of government policy: they provided a home to a little girl they fell in love with and whom their biological children considered a sibling. The youngest of this family, Brenda and Rebecca, are the girls in the cover image. And while there was nothing natural about how they became siblings, the love and joy between them is impossible to ignore.

Brenda tells the story of reconnecting with her white family. The young ones – Mark's daughters – prove pivotal in this. Their internet sleuthing and Facebook friend requests prove the bridge to the reconnection. One of those daughters, Kiara, gets a notification ping while in class and her teacher 'reminds her that she is in a history lesson'. Kiara replies, 'This is real history,' as she walks out. Later, she is able to confirm with Brenda that her white mum wants to see her.

Brenda's ability, with the help of her husband Mark, to blend a new family across culture and history – despite the intergenerational trauma – is another feature of this life story.

There are many moments in *The Last Daughter* that make a reader pause and reflect on the power of love and belonging. When Brenda and her mum uncover, with the help of Kim Burke, that they are Wiradjuri rather than Wailwan, it's a difficult adjustment to make. But after much work, Brenda is now comfortable saying she is a proud Wiradjuri woman.

'I can see her wrestling with this new information and who she thought she was all along,' writes Brenda of watching her mother in their moment of discovery. 'This is common for a lot of Indigenous people who were taken from their Country and placed somewhere else,' Kim tells them.

Reconnecting with Country and culture is part of Brenda's story. She learns the ancient art of weaving and works with Mark running camps on

Country, in northern New South Wales and southeast Queensland (with the endorsement of influential Indigenous figure Kyle Slabb from Fingal). This informs and deepens Brenda's strength of Aboriginality.

It is at one of these camps where Mark encourages Brenda to tell her story:

> I walk up to the line that Mark has drawn in the sand where he'd like me to stand, and I rub it out with my foot, drawing a new one a bit further back where I'm more comfortable. I am about to tell my story to strangers for the first time in my life. I'm fiddling with my hands and fingers. I take a deep breath and as the words start coming out of my mouth, memories come flooding back, and tears roll down my cheeks.

Countering lies and bearing witness

Finding voice, being heard and validated, is part of the human condition. *The Last Daughter* expresses it so well.

Brenda tells her story simply, with nothing exaggerated for effect. Known facts, recalled memory and renewed encounters are drawn together in spare, first-person prose. A memoir born from journal entries reproduced as exposition throughout, *The Last Daughter* is inspired by Brenda's need to know and share the truth.

She is motivated to counter lies about her parents, grandparents and great-grandparents – lies recorded as fact in government files. In just one example, the files record Brenda's mother requesting a photograph and progress report on Brenda while she was with her white family. It says these were supplied, but Brenda's mother never received anything. Even the date Brenda was returned to her family was incorrect.

Brenda's motivation increases when she and her siblings are excluded from formal recognition as being part of the stolen generations:

> The letter leaves me feeling like a microcosm of this land. It has been declared terra nullius – empty land – despite my people living here. Now my emotions, my memories, my trauma don't exist in the eyes of the government.

Brenda's pursuit of truth is reflected in the difficult conversations she has with herself, and with so many others in her Black, white, own (and eventually blended) family.

I can't fully imagine the courage, fear, heartache and dedication it took for Brenda to peel back the years and the layers to find truth for so many. The book is a project of love and reconnection.

Keeping everyone inside the warmth of that fire cannot have been easy. That fire and its warmth are offered with immense grace to readers – and now viewers – of Brenda's story. It is up to us to step inside that embrace and bear witness.

'He was horrific!' Nearly two-thirds of family historians are distressed by what they find. Should DNA kits come with warnings?

Susan Moore
Swinburne University of Technology

In 1853, my great-great-grandmother Charlotte died giving birth to her thirteenth child, in a tent on the banks of the Yarra River in what is now South Melbourne, but was then an overcrowded, muddy hellhole known as Canvas Town. The baby, William, died shortly afterwards. Researching Charlotte's story made me feel both sad for her loss and angry at the powerlessness of women's lives then.

I'm not the only one to have experienced intense emotions – both negative and positive – while researching my forebears. On Facebook pages, in media stories and on TV, you'll find a flood of hobby genealogists discovering shocking things about their ancestors – or even their own identity.

My April 2023 research revealed about two-thirds of family historians have experienced strong negative emotions such as sorrow or anger through their hobby. And nearly all respondents had experienced strong positive emotions such as joy or pride.

Passionate 'kin keepers'

In 2019, Doreen Rosenthal and I surveyed 775 Australian hobbyist family historians to examine their motivations. They were adults aged between twenty-one and ninety-three, but most were older and the median age was sixty-three. The majority (85 per cent) were women. This seems to be typical of hobbyist family historians. Women often take on the role of 'kin keeper', having the time to devote to it when they've finished rearing children and have retired from paid work.

Survey respondents described why they were passionately engaged with their hobby, and how it made them feel. Some 48 per cent 'sometimes' felt strong negative emotions about what they found, while 15 per cent did 'often'.

There were five common distress triggers.

1. Ancestors behaving badly

The first and most common distress trigger was the discovery of ancestors who had behaved badly, either as individuals or by profiting from unjust social conditions. Finding these forebears made family historians feel confronted, shocked and sometimes ashamed.

They said things like:

> [The worst thing was] finding the bigamist! He was horrific!! Very confronting thinking that I have some of his blood in my veins!

And from another:

> [It was] difficult finding that ancestors may have been involved in unsavoury behaviours or events. The problem is trying to understand the context of how they were able to do things that are socially and legally unacceptable today and not things I can be proud of.

2. Ancestors treated cruelly

It was also distressing to discover ancestors who had been cruelly treated. This elicited disturbing, even 'heartbreaking' feelings – and, at least implicitly, indignation at injustice. Many were deeply moved by what their ancestors experienced.

As one survey respondent put it:

> What is unexpected is the relationships that can be formed with those who are no longer with us. That I can be moved by the plight of my paternal step-great-great-grandmother who was incarcerated in a mental institution from 1913 to 1948 without review, without visitors, to get her out of the way.

3. Sad stories

Sadness was often specifically mentioned. As in the case of my great-great-grandmother who died in childbirth, sadness was usually a response to the hardships and tragedies ancestors faced in more challenging times.

Women commonly did not survive childbirth, neonatal deaths were frequent, and people died of diseases medical science has now conquered. Poverty was rife and war a constant threat.

One respondent said:

> [It was difficult] discovering the tragedies encountered by my Irish ancestors who came to Australia and their struggles and heartbreaking stories of survival for the next three generations.

Another said:

> [It is distressing] to uncover particularly sad and desperate times in some ancestors' lives. For example, a destitute widow who admitted her child to an orphan asylum for three years, only to have her child die of typhoid fever within two weeks of returning home.

4. Family secrets and betrayal

The fourth distress trigger was a belief by the family history researcher that they had been betrayed by other family members: through secrets, lies, and feeling their lived experience was ignored or denied.

This is particularly likely for those who discover 'secrets' about their parentage; for example, the late-life discovery of adoption, parental infidelity or previously unknown siblings. Trust is damaged. If family members can lie about these important things, what else might they lie about?

As one woman commented:

> My mother's half-sister did not accept that she shared a father with my mother. My great-grandmother lied about who my grandfather's father was. My great-great-grandmother also lied. All these lies were very distressing.

5. Moral dilemmas

Finally, several respondents expressed doubt and confusion at the moral dilemmas they faced on discovering information that could greatly distress other living relatives. Should they tell or not?

An emotional burden attaches to withholding potentially distressing information of this kind. Yet there is also guilt and fear about the possible outcomes of sharing it.

One person said:

> I knew an aunt had an illegitimate child before she married. Through DNA I found her granddaughter. I have yet to inform this girl who she is. I don't feel it's my right as she has absolutely no idea of any adoption of her father.

Another reported:

> A really distressing find was that my great-aunt's husband had committed a terrible murder. I have not been able to speak about this with the descendants of the couple.

Healthy outcomes from bad feelings

Sometimes, these distressing feelings can promote healthy, growth-enhancing outcomes. After the initial shock, some traumatic genealogical discoveries lead to a greater understanding of the past and its influence.

Placing ancestors' maladaptive or distressing behaviours, or their misfortunes, into historical and social context can help with acceptance and forgiveness, and stimulate emotional healing and personal growth. Initial feelings of distress about past injustices and tragedies are sometimes replaced by admiration for the strength and resilience of one's forebears. This can positively influence personal wellbeing and resilience.

How can family and professionals help?

I processed my great-great-grandmother's story by writing it down and sharing it with family members. We reworked our sadness at her fate into a positive family narrative, emphasising her bravery and the strengths her surviving children showed.

Support can mean just disclosing these stories to family members, friends and other family historians. But for some, it may be helpful to discuss these topics privately with a counsellor or therapist, especially if they've led to a breakdown in family relationships or an assault on one's sense of identity. Counsellors and psychologists should develop strategies to support clients distressed by genealogical findings, and encourage them to use their new-found knowledge for personal growth and greater understanding of family dynamics.

Should providers of genealogical research products (especially DNA tests) educate their customers about their products' potential to cause distress? Trigger warnings might be overkill, but they could issue lists of support resources for those who are upset or disoriented by their findings.

As more people gain access to more genealogical data, with the potential to challenge identity and uncover family secrets, it's worth thinking about.

Reviled, reclaimed and respected: The history of the word 'queer'

Timothy W Jones
La Trobe University

In recent years, a number of people have questioned or critiqued the use of the word 'queer' to describe LGBTQIA+ folk. For instance, one reader of *The Guardian* wrote a letter in January 2023 claiming that the 'q-word' was as derogatory and offensive as the 'n-word', and should not be used.

While there is a clear history of the word being used in aggressive and insulting ways, the meaning(s) and uses of 'queer' have never been singular, simple or stable.

The origin of the word 'queer'

'Queer' is a word of uncertain origin that had entered the English language by the early 16th century, when it was primarily used to mean 'strange', 'odd', 'peculiar' or 'eccentric'. By the late 19th century, it was being used colloquially to refer to same-sex-attracted men. While this usage was frequently derogatory, queer was simultaneously used in neutral and affirming ways.

The examples provided in the *Oxford English Dictionary* show this semantic range, including instances of homosexual men using queer as a positive self-description at the same time as it was being used in the most insulting terms. Compare the neutral: 'Fourteen young men were invited ... with the premise that they would have the opportunity of meeting some of the prominent "queers"' (1914). And the insulting: 'fairies, pansies, and queers conducted … lewd practices' (1936). And self-affirmed uses: 'young men who call themselves "queers"' (1952).

In the 1960s and 1970s, as sexual and gender minorities fought for civil rights and promoted new ways of being in society, we also sought new names for ourselves. Gay liberationists began to reclaim queer from its earlier hurtful usages, chanting 'out of the closets, into the streets', and singing 'we're here because we're queer'.

Their newsletters from the time reveal sustained questioning of the words, labels and politics of naming that lesbian and gay people could and should use about themselves. Some gay libbers even wanted to cancel the word 'homosexual' because they felt it limited their potential and 'prescribes a whole system of behaviour … which has nothing to do with my day-to-day living'.

In Australia, 'camp' was briefly the most common label that lesbian women and gay men used to describe themselves, before 'gay' became more prominent, used at that time by both homosexual men and women.

The evolving use of the word 'queer'

In the early 1990s, 'gay' had come to be used more typically to refer to gay men. Respectful and inclusive standards of language evolved to 'lesbian and gay', and then 'LGBT', as bisexuals and transgender people sought greater recognition. 'Queer' began to be used in a different way again: not as a synonym for 'gay', but as a critical and political identity that challenged normative ideas about sexuality and gender.

Queer theory drew on social constructionism – the theory that people develop knowledge of the world in a social context – to critique the idea any sexuality or gender identity was normal or natural. This showed how particular norms of sexuality and gender were historically contingent.

Thinkers such as Michel Foucault, Michael Warner, Judith Butler, Eve Kosofsky Sedgwick and Lauren Berlant were enormously influential in the development of this new idea of queer. Some people began to identify as queer in the critical sense, not as a synonym for a stable gender or sexual identity, but to indicate a non-conforming gender or sexual identity.

Activists in groups such as Queer Nation also used 'queer' in this critical sense as part of their more assertive, anti-assimilationist political actions.

'Queer' as an umbrella term

From the early 2000s, it became more common to use 'queer' as an umbrella term that was inclusive of the spectrum of sexual and gender identities represented in the LGBTQIA+ acronym. Today, 'queer' is included among the terms 'lesbian', 'gay', 'bisexual', 'transgender', 'gender diverse', 'intersex', 'asexual', 'brotherboy' and 'sistergirl', recognised in style guides as the most respectful and inclusive way to refer to people with diverse sexualities and genders.

Of course, the different usages and meanings of words such as 'queer' have often overlapped and been hotly contested. Historical usages and associations persist and can sit uncomfortably next to contemporary reclamations.

'Queer' as a slur?

Contemporary concerns with queer's historical use as a slur seem odd to me. The heritage report *A History of LGBTIQ+ Victoria in 100 Places and Objects*, which I co-authored, surveys the complexity of language use in historical and contemporary society.

It is notable that almost all of the words that LGBTQIA+ people use to describe ourselves today have been reclaimed from homophobic or transphobic origins. In fact, it could be said that liberating words from non-affirming religious, clinical or colloquial contexts and giving them our own meanings is one of the defining characteristics of LGBTQIA+ history.

While 'queer' does have a history of being used as an insult, that has never been its sole meaning. Same-sex-attracted and gender-diverse folks have taken the word and have been ascribing it with better meanings for at least the past fifty years. Queer's predominant use today is as an affirming term that is inclusive of all people in the rainbow acronym.

At a time when trans and gender-diverse folk are facing particularly harsh attacks, I'm all for efforts to promote inclusion and solidarity. Respectful language use doesn't require us to cancel 'queer', but rather to be mindful of its history and how that history is experienced by our readers and listeners.

Disability and dignity: Four things to think about if you want to 'help'

Angel Dixon
Griffith University
Elizabeth Kendall
Griffith University
Kelsey Chapman
Griffith University

The prevailing public perception is that everything people with disability do is a challenge. Sometimes, that is true. In those times, we may ask for or say 'yes' to a kind and respectful offer of assistance. Other times, and more often than not, we are simply navigating daily life when a person without disability interjects to offer assistance.

It is rare anyone means to be discriminatory in their approach to supporting people with disability, but society's attitude still has a way to go.

Disability rights activism used to take place in the streets or by occupying government property or buildings (sometimes, it still does). But the age of social media has created an opportunity for people with disability to explore and exercise advocacy in new ways, too. Air travel experiences of being treated – and handled – like 'baggage', as writer and advocate Zoe Simmons has detailed on Twitter, now known as X, expose the attitudinal barriers people with disability encounter when others 'help'.

There could be lots of reasons why people with disability decline or don't want offers of help. Recent research at the Dignity Project echoes Simmons's experience and also shows there is no 'one size fits all' approach to recommend.

But not offering assistance to fellow human beings is not the answer either. So, what is the right way to ask a person with disability if they would like help?

Disability is about the environment, not a diagnosis

More than 1.3 billion people globally live with disability. The Convention on the Rights of Persons with Disabilities states disability does not result from a diagnosis or impairment, but when a person encounters inaccessible, inflexible or insufficient environments, systems and attitudes.

In an ideal world, everyone would appreciate that disability is a mismatch between person and environment and would be motivated by a human rights perspective. In reality, Australian society is still lagging in its understanding of, and attitude towards, disability. Most people are confused or unsure about how to treat people with disability, which leads to exclusion and increases the barriers people with disability encounter.

Barriers for people with disability can be as obvious as a building with no elevator or as subtle as a pat on the back from a passer-by.

Barriers take their toll

Participants in the Dignity Project, a citizen science research and advocacy program at Griffith University, shared the impact and cumulative effect frequent and repeated encounters with barriers can have on a person's mental health and behaviour. These undignified interactions result in people feeling like 'less of a person, less worthy, less valid, less visible, annoyed, frustrated, sad, angry', with 'no rights, no voice, and reduced control'.

As a result, people may avoid social situations and isolate themselves. Over time, people with disability are silenced or diminished in their role as decision-makers in their own lives.

It can be useful to think about four aspects of offering help.

1. Acknowledge people and their rights

Misinformation and limited or reductive tropes perpetuated in the media contribute to the challenge of confronting and changing attitudes.

Participants in the Dignity Project called for acknowledgement and recognition that people with disability are human beings with the same full dimensions of personhood and human rights as people without disability. They described very few instances of needing help, but when they did, they said dignified experiences are defined by acknowledgement. In the words of one person:

> First off, ask me 'Do you need help?' and acknowledge that I might not need it. I will ask for help if I need it ... Ask how best to help and provide the help I ask for, rather than doing what [you think] I needed.

2. Pay attention to the response and consider what might be behind it

People with disability have rights, including the right to freedom of expression and opinion and respect for privacy. So, listen to a person's response when asked about needing assistance. If you receive a negative response, have empathy for what you may not necessarily understand. If a response is short or angry, accept it and don't grow resentful. That response may come from a history of discrimination and misrecognition.

The way to ask a person with disability if they would like help depends on contextual, subjective and relational factors. Providing help or support requires consideration of the diversity of experience, the situation, your relationship with the person and the consequences of helping or not helping.

Although helping may seem like an appropriate and polite thing to do, it may not even be appropriate to ask, particularly if doing so becomes a public act that draws attention to the person.

3. Know what not to do

There are some clear messages about what not to do, reiterated in our research and in Zoe Simmons's tweets.

Never physically touch someone, their assistive technology, aid or a support animal without asking.

It is inappropriate to ask people about their diagnosis or impairment if not related to the topic at hand, and make sure you use language that is dignified.

Even if you mean well, avoid comments that frame disability or a person's existence in a negative light, such as 'You're managing so well despite everything' or 'You're so brave'.

4. Think bigger

Social change takes time. Auditing your own personal biases while respectfully interacting with a person with disability, and simultaneously managing the mix of emotions that can be triggered by disability, is a complex social skill. Building an inclusive society will ensure people with and without disability can interact comfortably in the world together.

A positive and affirming form of 'help' might be ensuring environments and attitudes over which you have influence are always accessible and inclusive.

PART IX

Love and loss

Yunupiŋu was a great clan leader, a great family man and very much loved. I wish Australian political leaders could have learned more from him

Marcia Langton
University of Melbourne

Dr Yunupiŋu, who passed away in April on his Country in Arnhem Land at the age of seventy-four, was a magnificent person and a magnificent leader.

Most people in Australia who are aware of him know him as a ceremonial leader because of his towering presence leading ceremonies at the Garma Festival for so many years, and, most importantly, at events that he himself curated in order to make representations to prime ministers and ministers of Australian governments. Throughout his life, he had spoken and made representations to every prime minister of his adulthood.

He was a great clan leader, a great family man and very much loved by so many Australians who came into contact with him through his Garma Festival and so many other good works.

He was also an intellectual. He published some wonderful works, particularly *Tradition, Truth and Tomorrow*.

He was a musician, one of the most important traditional singers from northeastern Arnhem Land. Indeed, one could hear his beautiful voice on the *Tribal Voice* album, which his late younger brother's band Yothu Yindi made famous.

So many people will be in mourning for him. He touched so many people with his gracious leadership and kindness. It's such a shame, really, that he didn't live to see better outcomes.

Working for land rights

Constitutional recognition for Indigenous Australians was his idea. I was with him in Arnhem Land and he said to me, 'I want to see Noel Pearson.' They'd never met, and he told me to find Noel and get him to come and speak to him.

So, in those days, I had to drive around and find a Telstra hotspot. I found Noel. Noel jumped on a plane immediately and they met, and Yunupiŋu put to him constitutional recognition as a matter of highest importance. Because, as Yunupiŋu explains in his writings, he felt the existential threat towards his clan and other Indigenous people.

He was the interpreter for the clan leaders in the Aboriginal Land Rights Commission, appointed by Gough Whitlam to determine how land rights were to be recognised. He had been appointed by his father to become a clan leader and to go through the many years of learning that involved.

By interpreting for all the clan leaders and their evidence, he became extremely knowledgeable. He also interpreted in the court in Canberra in the *Milirrpum* native title case. Later, of course, when the *Land Rights Act* had passed and the land councils were established, he became chair of the Northern Land Council and served in that position twice.

So, he is, in many ways, one of the crucial figures in the land rights movement. He was able to translate philosophical beliefs and the inherited ancient property systems of Yolŋu people to a very wonderful judge, Justice Edward Woodward, to enable a land rights system to be legislated.

He also contributed to culture, the survival of Aboriginal culture, and to education. The Yothu Yindi Foundation press release on his passing explains how he initiated the Dhupuma Barker School in his community in Arnhem Land, which has been producing wonderful results, with high attendance rates for the children.

He also led many other initiatives – too many to mention. People turned to him for advice because of his highly honed political and strategic skills.

A kind man

The great quality he had was kindness. He chose not to make people his enemy, unless they'd committed some egregious crime. He always attempted to find humanity in people. He was able to speak to every prime minister, as I've said, and encourage Indigenous leaders to set goals – such as constitutional recognition – and find a way to achieve them.

He pulled together the clans of Arnhem Land and presented three petitions on constitutional recognition to prime ministers Julia Gillard and Kevin Rudd. He was very determined about this. He also gave some wonderful lectures on this topic.

Many people have been inspired by him because he always found a way through the terrible burden of colonialism. Nobody suffered it more than people like himself.

There is a terrible view, sometimes, that traditional people were not affected by colonialism. That's far from the truth. In fact, I think if any Indigenous culture survives today, and of course so much does, it is precisely because people like this great man valued culture above all else.

He took his ceremonial responsibilities as the highest priority and he regarded the survival of his own culture, and by extension other Indigenous cultures, as matters of the highest importance. Because it is in our cultures that we find the values that make life worthwhile, make life worth living, and enable us to enjoy life.

And he did enjoy life. He had a wonderful life. It's such a tragic loss for everyone.

I met him in the late 1970s and we became very good friends and remained so throughout our lives. He was very curious, a great intellectual, and I believe he had a huge concern, not only for his family, but also for the friends he made far and wide.

Hence the popularity of the Garma Festival, with so many people from Australia and around the world. He truly believed that we are all one people; we all have red blood running through our veins.

I wish Australian political leaders could have learned more from him, because Australia would be so much better as a country if they had adopted some of his values. He certainly showed the way forward.

Editor's note: Yunupiŋu's family have given permission for his name to be used in this article.

'When my thoughts would stray over the sea': Reading the 19th-century diaries of girls migrating to Australia

Catherine Gay
University of Melbourne

In the digital age, our lives are constantly being recorded. Yet the deliberate act of recording – what we want to remember and how we want to remember it – remains popular. Diaries allow us to journal our thoughts and feelings, to work through the challenges we face every day.

This practice is older than you may think. As I write in my journal article of May 2023, some British and Irish girls and young women who migrated to Australia in the mid-1800s used diaries to record their day-to-day lives, document their travel experiences and navigate their emotions.

In the 19th century, around 1.5 million people migrated to Australia, including large numbers of girls, who were defined as under the age of fifteen, and young women in their late teens and early twenties. Unless she was married, a girl had little other option than to accompany her family to the colonies. Though few diaries from this demographic survive (I examine only thirteen extant sources of about 850 known to exist), they divulge the intricate emotions of migration.

Today, a 24-hour flight from Britain to Australia feels like an eternity, but in the 19th century it took around three months to sail to the continent. Removed from the demands of everyday life, passengers had a lot of time on their hands. Some wrote journals to while away the long days.

A difficult experience

Migration could be a difficult experience. Passengers endured months at sea in cramped conditions, often fearing for their safety and health. They missed those left behind and worried about their futures in a new land. It is such thoughts and emotions that can be found in surviving migrant girls' diaries.

Aboard the *Great Victoria* in 1864, 22-year-old Isabella Adcock had to share cramped cabins with strangers and complained about it in her journal. She had 'feelings repugnance to the sleeping accommodations and indeed almost everything in the ship'.

Diaries were sometimes a mechanism to cope with boredom and frustration. Jane Swan, thirteen, was impatient to reach Australia in 1853. She was sick of the 'very long voyage' and felt that 'to see the same things, and the same faces, becomes very tiresome'.

Working-class girls were subject to strict conditions. On her voyage to Brisbane in 1863, fourteen-year-old Welsh girl Maria Steley noted in her diary that 'young women are put Down every night at six O clock' and 'are not Allowed to speak to the young men'.

Diary of Maria Steley
Source: John Oxley Library, State Library of Queensland.

As a working-class teenager, Maria was separated from her family and housed with the single women. Wealthier girls would stay with their families in private cabins.

Among such shared conditions, girls could also make friends. Maria wrote she and her new pals 'have many bits of fun more than i thought we would' by 'singing and Dancing and playing eney thing we like untill 10 O clock then we go to bed we Play four howrs after we are Loch Down'. (Spelling mistakes are per the original.)

But shipboard travel generated loneliness for many girls. Working-class Scottish woman Mary Maclean, who was twenty-two when she voyaged to Sydney in 1865, experienced homesickness, often 'Sheding a tear and often Wonder if thay miss one at Home'.

Joy and sadness

Girls also used diaries to record their fears. Illness, for one thing, could tear through the close confines of a ship. Sarah Raws, who was fifteen when she sailed to Melbourne in 1854, was preoccupied with the proximity of death, including that of two infant boys and the 'very sudden' death of a lady in Sarah's own cabin.

Emily Braine, ten years old when she embarked in 1854, was 'frightened' by large waves and rough seas. The risk of shipwreck was low, but the possibility played on Emily's mind.

Towards the end of their journey, some girls were excited to disembark. Sarah Raws rejoiced 'when we first saw land' from the ship's deck. But others experienced a resurgence of homesickness and doubt.

Nearing Melbourne in 1874, nineteen-year-old Ally Heathcote had feelings 'of a mingled character, joy and sadness'. She felt torn between her old life in England and her new life in Victoria. Ally's writings helped her deal with these 'mingled' feelings. Her diary, she wrote,

> has helped to keep me employed during the passage and many times I have turned to it when my thoughts would stray over the sea, and have written the account of the day's proceedings when otherwise I should have begun to mope.

Most girls concluded their diaries at the end of their voyage, before they started on a new life. Some made copies and sent the accounts 'home' to Britain for family and friends to peruse. The diary became a record and a keepsake of a life-changing journey.

Girls' shipboard diaries reveal the complex and varied emotions of people from the past and provide insight into the human experience of migration. These sources centre girls in the migration narrative, giving a voice to an often-overlooked group.

It is a shame so few survive.

Love in the time of incontinence. Why young people don't have a monopoly on love, or even sex

Carol Lefevre
University of Adelaide

A friend with a close relative in a residential aged-care home reports, in a tone of scandalised surprise, on romantic entanglements among the elderly. In one case, a man and woman have become so inseparable that staff have been forced to move his bed into her room so the two can sleep side by side. When the woman's son made an unexpected visit, he was distressed to find his mother in her nightdress in the arms of a stranger, though eventually he had to accept it was what she wanted.

The concept of the elderly, with their age-altered bodies, demonstrating an appetite for intimacy, especially in an institutionalised setting, appears widely regarded as funny at best – and at worst, disgusting. But should we be surprised if, in this difficult, final phase of their lives, elderly people yearn for human contact?

Love is so short, forgetting is so long

As another friend, an experienced nurse, points out, the rooms of aged-care residents are routinely lined with framed family photographs – what she calls 'the people with the big hats and the scrolls'. But where, my friend demands, are these people in the lives of the lonely residents? Why do they never visit?

She describes how in her childhood in Ireland, any house you'd go to would have an old man or woman in it being cared for by the family; though she admits this may no longer be the case, since so many women have found work outside the home.

For Australians in aged care, living among strangers, removed from all that was once familiar – including the ordinary luxuries of an outing to a local cafe, or to watch the sun set over the sea – it is surely natural that they should turn to those nearest them for comfort. As the poet Pablo Neruda said: 'Love is so short, forgetting is so long.'

Each February, the Day of Love rolls around, with its buckets of poor, forced roses outside florists' shops, its gaudy greetings cards and supermarkets crammed with chocolate. Young people, of course, are mad for all the hullabaloo, with Valentine's Day–themed parties, and singing telegrams delivered in the lunch breaks in high schools. But if those young people imagine they have a monopoly on love, or even on sex, the truth appears otherwise – in real life and in books.

Romance in residential care

For a moving narrative of love at the end of days, read Alice Munro's 'The Bear Came Over the Mountain', from her book *Hateship, Friendship, Courtship, Loveship, Marriage* (filmed as *Away from Her*; director Sarah Polley was Oscar-nominated for her screenplay adaptation of Munro's story). The story documents both romantic attachment in residential care and the lengths a spouse might go to for love.

Grant and Fiona have been married for almost fifty years when she starts leaving sticky notes on their kitchen drawers: 'Cutlery', 'Dishtowels', 'Knives'. Grant is shaken by the realisation that it is not where things are kept that Fiona is struggling with, but what they are.

As Fiona's memory loss accelerates, she moves voluntarily to Meadowlake, a nursing home where she and Grant have previously visited a neighbour. The home's rules forbid visitors during the first month; Grant is told this is to help Fiona settle in. But when the month is up, his wife does not recognise him, and at each visit he finds her sitting close beside her new friend, Aubrey.

Grant's eventual acceptance of Fiona and Aubrey's relationship, and his efforts, after Aubrey's wife takes him home, to have him returned to Meadowlake, is where the real love lies in this story. It is not the stuff of cellophane-wrapped roses and chocolate hearts, but the devotion that has accreted over the course of a long marriage. In Grant's case, devotion may be tinged with guilt, for in the past he has been a philanderer – though he never wanted to risk losing his wife. Now that he has lost her, he throws his effort into securing the only thing that appears to make her happy.

At the end of Elizabeth Strout's Pulitzer Prize–winning *Olive Kitteridge*, Olive seeks out the widowed Jack Kennison. She puts her hand on his chest and feels the thump of his heart, 'and her body – old, big, sagging – felt straight-out desire for his'. Olive is saddened to remember she had not loved her husband Henry in this way for a long time before he died.

> What young people didn't know, she thought, lying down beside this man, his hand on her shoulder, her arm; oh, what young people did not

know. They did not know that lumpy, aged, and wrinkled bodies were as needy as their own young, firm ones, that love was not to be tossed away carelessly.

Privacy, consent and family resistance

Intimate relationships have been associated with lower levels of stress and depression; with higher levels of oxytocin, a feel-good hormone; and a general lift in physical and mental wellbeing, even taking into account cognitive or physical impairment.

Intimacy, of course, does not necessarily mean sex. It can be expressed through touch, such as hugging, cuddling or hand-holding. But in an Australian aged-care setting, this may not be as straightforward as it seems in fiction. For one thing, there is a discouraging lack of privacy, including a scarcity of shared rooms, rooms with double beds and lockable doors. Then, if a resident's husband or wife is still living in the wider community, a new attachment might stir family resistance.

A 2022 survey of almost 3000 Australian residential aged-care facilities, conducted by researchers at La Trobe University's Australian Centre for Evidence Based Aged Care, found that only half had written policies on sexuality, and only one-third had policies on sexual behaviour.

Dementia raises the question of a capacity to properly consent. Legislation is clear concerning a resident's will and medical and financial matters. But when it comes to people's sexual decisions, it is left to staff to negotiate a balance between the rights of individuals and the facility's duty of care to a group of people who are particularly vulnerable to unwanted attentions, or even sexual assault.

It must be acknowledged that in Australia, an estimated fifty sexual assaults occur every week in residential aged care, and that the elderly also experience such assaults in their own homes; the victims are invariably female. Police and care providers can be unwilling to take action, believing that dementia makes the victim's evidence unreliable – and, mistakenly, that people with dementia will not remember, nor be traumatised.

The Ready to Listen project, launched in 2021 by the Older Persons Advocacy Network, aims to address the rights of people in aged care to be heard, to be believed, and (following open disclosure of assault) to have their cases followed up by police. It is also concerned with establishing a charter of sexual rights for older people, including their right to a consenting, romantic relationship, and clarifying the all-important question of consent.

But the possibility of non-consensual contact exacerbates the difficulty of forming genuine attachments, and family disapproval may be enough to cause staff to intervene. Even without this, the lack of guidance, or the ageist prejudices of staff members, may mean intimate friendships within an aged-care setting will be firmly discouraged.

Children, especially adult children, can complicate mature love, and are often unscrupulous in thwarting it. Because aside from what they perceive as age-appropriate behaviour, late-life attachments can, of course, have consequences for an offspring's anticipated inheritance.

'You're not even ashamed'

In Kent Haruf's *Our Souls at Night*, Addie Moore and Louis Waters, neighbours for years, both live alone – their houses empty of family, their evenings solitary. Then Addie visits Louis with the astonishing proposal that he sleep over with her at night: for the company, for the quiet conversations after lights out. Louis agrees, and they fall into a companionable routine. The town soon notices this new intimacy, but, at seventy, Addie does not care what anyone thinks, and nor does Louis.

Alerted by a friend to her father's behaviour, Louis's daughter Holly tells him, 'It just seems embarrassing.' But Addie's son Gene is incensed. 'Because he's after your money too, isn't he?' he says. 'If you married him he'd get half of everything, wouldn't he? I couldn't stop him.'

Addie's six-year-old grandson Jamie is sent to stay with her when Gene separates from his wife. Frightened at night, Jamie ends up sleeping in Addie's bed, making her arrangement with Louis impossible. But gradually the three of them bond, and when Louis gives Jamie a dog, Bonny, Bonny is allowed to sleep on Jamie's bed. When the three of them go camping, they share the same tent.

Gene comes and takes Jamie and Bonny away, and afterwards Addie and Louis decide they will do what the town believes they've been doing all along. Addie says, 'This old body. I'm an old woman now.' Louis says, 'Well, old woman Moore. You've won me completely. You're just right. You're how you're supposed to look.'

When their lovemaking is not a success, Louis says, 'I've got the old man's complaint.' Addie says, 'It's just the first time. We have all the time ahead of us … Let's try again another night.' But Addie's son returns. 'I want this to stop,' he says. 'You're not even ashamed of yourselves.'

Gene bans Addie from speaking on the phone to her grandson. When she does get through to Jamie, he tells her that if he talks to her, 'they'll take Bonny away'. Addie must have contact with the boy; she cannot afford to wait until Jamie is sixteen. She tells Louis they must remain separate.

When Addie falls in the street, Gene has her transferred from the town of Holt, where she and Louis live, to Denver. Louis goes to the hospital, where Gene tells him, 'You're not wanted here.'

When Addie is discharged, she will move into assisted living in another town. Gene's disgust, while partly motivated by financial need, is also an expression of a common distaste for age-altered bodies. To Gene, this is all the justification he needs to use his small son as a weapon.

Love after 'fifty years of being parched'

Addie Moore is not the first elderly woman to discover that the last great love of her life is settled on a grandchild. The unconditional love can flow both ways, to their mutual joy, if it is not pinched out by parents with a loveless attitude towards the older generation. In her surrealist novel *The Hearing Trumpet*, Leonora Carrington delivers this dehumanising impulse with devastating economy as a woman speaks to her husband about his aged mother, Marian.

'Remember, Galahad,' added Muriel, 'those old people do not have feelings like you or I. She would be so much happier in an institution.' Unfortunately for Marian, her adult grandson is not the loving kind. 'She ought to be dead,' Robert said. 'At that age people are better off dead.'

Even when offspring are not primarily focused on their inheritance, a lifetime's accumulation of feelings and resentments can be in play. In *Anything is Possible*, also by Elizabeth Strout, the story 'Mississippi Mary' tells of a 78-year-old woman living in Italy, married to a man so much younger than her that at first the locals assumed she was his mother.

When her youngest daughter visits, Mary thinks she will not understand 'what it had been like to be so famished. Almost fifty years of being parched.' At their fiftieth wedding anniversary party, her husband had not asked her to dance. Later, when Mary was sixty-nine, her daughters had given her a trip to Italy as a birthday gift, and it was there that she had wandered off and become lost, and was found by Paolo.

She fell in love. She did. He'd been married for twenty years, it had seemed like fifty to him, and now he was alone – they were both parched.

Mary's first husband had been in a long-term affair. Their daughter Angelina judges it 'pathetic … painful, of course, but pathetic'. Her father 'really was a mean snake of a man', Angelina admits, but then the selfishness of the hurt child kicks in:

> Why couldn't her mother see what she had done by leaving? Why couldn't she see it? There could be only one reason: that her mother was, behind her daffiness, a little bit dumb; she lacked imagination.

Angelina accuses her mother of having taken from her the ability to care for her in her old age, and to be with her when she dies. Mary is a little stricken by this, because she suspects death is not far away. But 'she did not dread her death … she was almost ready for it, not really but getting there'. Mary admits that:

> Always, there was that grasping for a few more years, Mary had seen this with many people, and she did not feel it – or she did, but she did not. No. She felt tired out, she felt almost ready, and she could not tell her child this.

Sexy old women

In her essay 'Sexy Old Women', Krissy Kneen has just finished writing a novel that will go on to be shortlisted for the Stella Prize, *An Uncertain Grace*, in which the main character, Liv, reaches 130 years of age and is still very much a sexual being. Kneen writes:

> The older I get the more I see that the signifiers of sex are inextricably linked to youth. We say young, sexy bodies. We say sexy young things. We do not say sexy old woman.

In the work of writers such as Gabriel Garcia Márquez, Philip Roth, Yasunari Kawabata, Michel Houellebecq, Peter Carey and Vladimir Nabokov, Kneen easily finds literary examples of sexual old men. But it is harder to find a model for a sexual older woman, and in the few examples she does find – *In Praise of the Stepmother* by Mario Vargas Llosa and *The Graduate* by Charles Webb (the basis for the 1967 film starring

Dustin Hoffman) – the women are portrayed as 'dangerous, manipulating, clever enough to cause a man's downfall'.

Kneen recalls watching the screening of a documentary, *Nitrate Kisses*, in which a sex scene involving two very old women draws a shocked response from the young audience. Describing the scene as 'caring and quite frankly, beautiful', Kneen, though at the time still young herself, hopes that as an old woman she will still be 'equally sexually bold'.

Ripe glamour

Septuagenarian American novelist and poet May Sarton famously developed the optimistic concept of 'ripening towards death in a fruitful way'. But ripeness as it relates to the elderly, especially elderly women, can be a fraught topic. Some pro-ageing advocates insist that an essential element of a woman ageing well is glamour, but glamour is a construct. In our times, it is often measured by the subject's perceived sexual appeal, as demonstrated by the clichéd poses and facial expressions of those modelling 'glamour' in magazines or on screens.

The pro-ageing movement on Instagram is divided between older women who still lay claim to the glamorous props of their youth – skin-baring garments, high heels, extravagant quantities of make-up – and those who are evolving towards a kind of beauty that does not rely on overt sexuality, but focuses instead on being comfortable in one's own skin. Neither approach is right or wrong, but of the two ways of going forward, the 'less is more' philosophy of the natural agers somehow seems more universally doable.

The roots of the word 'glamour' can be traced to the Scottish word *gramarye*, meaning 'magic, enchantment, spell', including the lovely phrase 'to cast the glamour'. *Gramarye* may be from an Ancient Greek word for the weight unit of ingredients used in magic potions. Or is it an alteration of the English word 'grammar', in its medieval sense of 'scholarship' and especially 'occult learning'?

In John Jamieson's 1825 *Etymological Dictionary of the Scottish Language*, *glamer* is

> the supposed influence of a charm on the eye, causing it to see objects differently from what they really are. Hence to 'cast glamer o'er one, to cause deception of sight'.

This definition draws glamour closer to the Old Norse words *glámr*, 'moon', or 'name of a ghost', and *glámsýni*, 'illusion' – which makes of glamour a deception, a beauty trick.

Jamieson's dictionary contains many old words that women might use to describe themselves in ways that stand outside the conventions formed around youthful beauty. For those of us anticipating our own extreme old age, when we will be more *frooch* ('frail, brittle') than now, let us hope we shall still be able to summon the odd moment of *gleit* ('to glitter'), and that our eyes, our hair, will be touched at times with their old *glister* ('lustre').

And looking back over the fiction I've drawn on for this essay, I see the writers were both *forsy* ('powerful') and *formois* ('beautiful').

The right to relationships

The Royal Commission into Aged Care Quality and Safety was announced by the Morrison government in 2018, following a string of disturbing incidents – including South Australia's Oakden aged-care scandal, where the facility was closed after evidence came to light of neglect and abuse. Among the findings of the royal commission were that 'sub-standard care and abuse pervades the Australian aged care system'. In its final report, it pronounced this 'a source of national shame'.

Reforms suggested by the royal commission in any overhaul of Australia's aged-care system include the right of autonomy, the right to the presumption of legal capacity, and in particular the right of elders in residential aged care to make decisions about their care and the quality of their lives, and the right to social participation.

The recommendations state that older people should be supported to exercise choice about their own lives and make decisions to the fullest extent possible, including being able to take risks and be involved in the planning and delivery of their care. They also state that older people are entitled to receive support that acknowledges the aged-care setting is their home, and enables them to live in security, safety and comfort, with their privacy respected.

For those of us who are not yet quite ready to access these late-life services, let us hope the Albanese government follows through on the royal commission's recommendations, which state that people should be treated as individuals. And that the relationships older people have with significant others in their lives should be acknowledged, respected and fostered.

Private Leo, my imaginary father

Kevin John Brophy
University of Melbourne

My mother fell in love with my father, Leo, at a suburban Melbourne dance hall in 1946. He was twenty-six, handsome, athletic, smart, a newly minted war veteran, and his grin was infectious. They were a dazzling couple, as their later wedding photos show. Many decades on, my mother liked to tell of Leo's mother warning her that he was going to prove a handful, and was she prepared for this? Possibly my mother told the story to let us know that her love for Leo could never be doubted. Or equally she might have been letting us know that she had no idea what a handful he would actually turn out to be.

In 2017, when Leo died at the age of ninety-seven, one of my brothers gave me a folder of papers. They were the documents of our father's military service. I put them away with clippings, incomplete family trees, photos, and birth and marriage certificates that constitute a patchy record of our unwritten family history.

Three years later, at the height of Melbourne's extended lockdowns against a rising death toll from COVID, with time on my hands at home, I began going through the bookshelves, throwing out what would never be read or consulted again, and culling papers accumulated through forty years of writing and teaching. I found forgotten letters from past lovers and exchanges arising from past close friendships in whole series of letters – reminders that once I'd been a young man with hopes and ideals, but no idea what the future held for that young man. There were letters and notes from my father, too, one of them dismissing me as a 'receiver'. His disappointments in me were many. His letter explained at length what a receiver is on the football field and how teammates feel about such a cowardly player among them.

When I came across his war documents this time, it was with a fresh curiosity about the young man who had been the subject of eight years of military clerks' scribbled notes. I wondered how I might fit this record of him as a young recruit to the violent father I'd known. As his first son and second child, I had swum in a world made of him, never wondering whether I really knew him but always feeling I knew him too well. Perhaps, I thought now, in these military records I might glimpse the youth he once was.

I can remember a line of white rime along the edge of his mouth as he beat me one night, seemingly unable to stop, my mother from the hallway saying over and over, 'That's enough, Leo.' What strikes me now is that I so neatly filed away this image of his lips during the terror of a beating.

Sometimes, there were lucky escapes when he did hold himself back. We had a square wooden table painted blue that fitted into a kitchen alcove. It was possible to scramble under this table as a small child and press myself against the far wall out of his reach, knowing he would refuse the indignity of getting down on his knees to crawl in after me.

Going through the papers of his war record, I began to wonder if he was someone else as a young man – someone I would not have feared and might have even enjoyed knowing.

In his late teenage years, wiry Leo was a talented suburban cricketer, about average height, with a thin, straight nose and that handsome grin. His intense green eyes were too deeply set to ever give him an expression of openness, though in certain moods he would have been handsome and irresistible.

A week before turning nineteen, in the inner-northern Melbourne suburb of Carlton, he enlisted in the Australian armed forces, signing an oath to 'well and truly serve Australia's Sovereign Lord the King' for the next three years. This was seven months before Australia joined with Britain in war. Too young for the army, Leo had enlisted in the mostly part-time Citizens Militia Force, a body meant to supply the army with trained recruits. Once war was declared in September 1939, 40,000 were immediately deployed from the militia into full service. Was Leo declaring himself keen to be part of that war once it got underway?

I don't understand this enthusiasm to be absorbed into the military so early. Perhaps it was a way of putting distance between himself and his childhood family. Or something he did with his mates in a moment of shared restless ratbaggery. It might have been a sign of determination to show his older brothers he had become a man. Among them, Jim and Bernie did not enlist until 1942.

Leo was one of six brothers, and as it turned out he would be the only one among them not to achieve a professional education. Suddenly enlisting at eighteen might have been the beginning of a series of impulsive decisions that so complicated his life, it became impossible for him to stop improvising as he went, decade after decade, through the rest of the 20th century.

Not once did I hear from him a word of praise for England or the English. With an identity built upon Irish Catholic hatred directed at Great Britain, he could not have joined the military in the hope of being sent to Europe to defend the English.

But even so, in November 1941, he signed a new form in Carlton to enlist as a regular soldier. One part he left blank, possibly as self-protection: what is your religious denomination? Control of what he considered personal information was always vital to him.

Less than a year later he signed a further attestation, this time from an office at Adelaide River, a hundred kilometres south of Darwin. He noted on this form that he had been serving as a corporal at an Australian Army Bulk Issue Petrol and Oil Depot in the Northern Territory. He committed to serving the king 'until the cessation of the present time of war and twelve months thereafter'. His Medical Examination Report is a quick handwritten note: 'A1.' He left education and religion details blank. He was moved to Darwin.

He had been serving in the Northern Territory since the first week of April 1942, and by then the Japanese air force had made ten raids on Darwin and across the Territory, including a bombing of Katherine, 300 kilometres inland. Beginning in June 1942, the bombing raids over Darwin included low-level strafing by Japanese Zeroes. The long-range Zero fighter planes, stripped of armour and radios, were so lightweight, fast and deadly that pilots of the less nimble Australian planes each carried a pocket-map marking food caches buried along the northern coast in case they were shot down – as many were.

Much later, my father recounted that the troops in Darwin became so familiar with the routines and flight paths of the Japanese bombing fleets that they knew what times were good for being out on patrol or out partying, and when to head for the bunkers near the beach.

There were at least seventy-seven raids over the Northern Territory alone between 1942 and 1944. Nearly 200 Japanese airmen died as their planes were brought down, with many wrecks and bodies still not found today. By my count, my father was present for more than thirty raids during his eleven months in and around Darwin.

In his eighties, he became somewhat deaf, and blamed this on the effects of being so close to exploding Japanese bombs. There were stories of him leaving a card game just before a bomb landed, and of raiding the liquor cabinets in abandoned suburban Darwin houses, wheeling out a piano to dance and sing in the empty streets between raids. When he was in his nineties, and I was spending time in Halls Creek, he said that if he had got there during his service in the north it would have been in the back of a military police truck under arrest, since Halls Creek was the site of the army's prison.

My impression is of a restless man moving step by step, oath by oath, deeper into the army, further from home, and closer to harm. He was never the kind of patriot to be proud of dying for his military leaders or his nation, but perhaps he was the kind of young man who could not resist an adventure, a chance to prove himself, or a shot at being among the bravest. He could have remained safely a clerk at the Adelaide River Depot, but it seems he was determined to be in Darwin under those bombs.

Leo had a younger brother after whom I was named. He was disabled by polio; I have seen a newspaper photo of the older brothers wheeling him on a portable bed to a Victorian Football League (VFL) game. His illness might have been rare bad luck, but not so rare then that the family felt singled out by a malevolent fate. He died aged seventeen in 1940. There is one small, glossy snapshot of him peeking over the top of his wicker pram, head propped by a fluffed pillow, a confident smile across his thin face, his gaze direct. In this photo, he looks as if he would take an interest in whoever stopped to talk. He looks well loved.

My father's parents, Alice and Tom, were stalwart members of their community and their Catholic parish. Alice had been a schoolteacher. Tom was a local station master in the inner-northern Melbourne suburb of Coburg after serving in country towns. He kept a milking cow on Crown land beside his railway station. In a surviving family photo, he stands in a railway uniform ramrod straight, unsmiling and clear-eyed in front of his extended family. My father never spoke about him except to tell the story of his death.

Tom died at the age of sixty-six, in 1947, fallen from his bicycle in Princes Park on his way home from the Carlton football ground. That afternoon, the Carlton team had made a grand comeback in muddy conditions from being five goals adrift of Richmond well into the third quarter. Carlton would go on to win the VFL premiership that year, with their centre-halfback Bert Deacon securing the Brownlow Medal.

When Tom failed to return, my newly married father and one of his brothers went out looking through Brunswick and around Princes Park. Eventually, they went to the Carlton police station, where they were told that there was an unidentified body at the city morgue. The brothers late that night identified the body of their father. He had died of a heart attack.

I wonder about Leo as a 27-year-old identifying the anonymous body of his father only a few years after brothers on both sides of him had died, and himself a recent war survivor.

It was the death of the third son, Bernie, early in the battles of Finschhafen on the remote Huon Peninsula in the north of New Guinea that, I think, most deeply shook my father. Bernie died in October 1943 at the age of twenty-six, one of seventy-three Australians to die in the first of those battles. The record shows my father was given a week's leave without pay shortly after Bernie's death, then a second request for another week of leave was rejected. A few months later, he changed his 'next of kin' notice on his military details from his mother's to his father's name. The telegram notice of Bernie's death had been delivered directly to his mother, and I guess Leo understood that she could not have withstood another such telegram.

In his last years, my father asked to be taken to Papua New Guinea to visit Bernie's grave at the Lae War Cemetery. No-one in the family had been there, and as the last living brother, his mind went to this unfinished business. But he weakened too much and too quickly for us to consider the journey.

His other older brother Jim flew bomber planes across Germany from Britain. Afterwards, Jim kept his medals out of sight. Refusal to celebrate the war might have been a necessary family gesture of respect for the death of Bernie.

My father's military mementos lived in the spidery stillness of a dim shed at the back of our childhood yard in Coburg. I remember a jacket with corporal stripes, a sheathed Japanese bayonet that I spent many hours polishing and marvelling over. And a gasmask of rubber and canvas that turned my brothers and me into monsters as we took turns trying it on.

On 11 January 1943, Leo's papers show he was demoted from corporal to private at his own request. He had joined the First Australian Parachute Battalion. Without direct combat experience, and by concealing a defect that would have excluded him, he had managed to be selected for the most elite fighting and flying unit ever formed in Australia. His defect was colour blindness.

His story was that he listened to a man in front give answers to the questions on colour vision, memorised them on the spot, and repeated them back to the testing officer. Did he do this for a bet or just for the hell of it? Or was he caught up in some kind of trouble, and this voluntary demotion with a switch to the new paratroop battalion looked to be a way out? And if perception of colour might have meant the difference between life and death on the battlefield for himself and his comrades, why did he risk such disaster? His paths through the army and the war look to me to be erratic, impulsive, risky.

As a member of the First Parachute Battalion, newly private Leo was being trained to make incursions into enemy territories. As well as airborne drills, the men were expected to learn guerrilla warfare tactics while carrying on their backs equipment weighing up to 30 kilograms. He qualified as a parachutist in December 1943, which meant he had completed at least seven successful jumps over ten months, a time cleaved by the death of his brother Bernie.

Refusals to jump were not uncommon among trainees. Most often, this occurred on a trainee's third flight. The explanation for this was that a first jump could be exhilarating, the second a return to reality, then at the third, a man might come to understand the real dangers. These troops jumped without auxiliary parachutes on the reasoning that the auxiliary pack was too cumbersome, and in any case, they were jumping at such low heights that if a parachute failed there would be no time to release an auxiliary.

Within the first year of the formation of the Parachute Battalion, five men had died in training mishaps and more had suffered broken limbs, concussion and other injuries. The parachutists soon won rights to extra pay in recognition of risk and danger. These superbly fit and now well-paid young men became infamous for excursions to whatever breweries, hotels and brothels were near their remote bush training grounds.

To be a paratrooper was to know that you might at any time be ordered to jump out into an enemy sky, an easy floating target for snipers. With one son dead in New Guinea, another training for high-casualty missions, and a third flying bomber planes over Europe, this family must have seemed set to pay much too high a price for any coming Allied victory.

In March 1944, the Parachute Battalion underwent intensive jungle warfare manoeuvres, participated in dawn attack rehearsals over Wollongong, and were moved from the Blue Mountains to Mareeba in North Queensland, not far inland from Cairns, in preparation for a possible mission into New Guinea with American support. It was during this month of feverish preparations for real engagement in the war that my father suffered injuries to his ankles in a jump. He was one of five injured in training jumps during that month. Leo was hospitalised at Concord on the Parramatta River, where he was treated, then discharged to the Lady Gowrie Convalescent Home. From April until July, he was moved between hospital and convalescent home repeatedly. It seemed he was being invalided out of the army.

Somehow, though, and following his own brand of determination, he found his way back to the Parachute Battalion's training ground in Queensland, where he took charge of managing the officers' mess. JB Dunn notes in his history of the paratroopers that, at this time, Leo had earned the reputation of being 'the most tight-lipped man in the Battalion'.

He had made his way back north, I imagine, because he had found for himself a place and a reputation among these paratroopers. Privy to information, accepted by this species of men, and probably at least on the fringes of whatever scams went on, Leo could be trusted to keep the truth close. This fits the man I knew. He loved to talk, and he could have his audience in his hands at the dinner table once he turned his talents to mocking our neighbours and friends. But when it came to business or money or murkier matters of sexuality, he was either utterly tight-lipped or so meanderingly impenetrable in anything he said that I could not trust or follow his talk.

Operating from a zone of bluff somewhere between bully and charmer, salesman and commander, he never let up. I expect in business he wore people down. He was always looking to show us he was a man with the inside information, the man with a way through where others floundered. When he wanted one of my younger brothers to be privately tutored in mathematics, he found a man a few doors away who was so smart 'he could teach a cow to count'.

My brother was sent to him for lessons and I was encouraged to go there, too, to play chess with this apparently brilliant man. I don't know why I agreed to go. A deep introvert as teenage years approached, I spent my days when I could with comics and books. Perhaps I went out of curiosity, or most likely it was just easier to do what my father told me to do.

This amazing man my father had found lived in a small, newly built house with a young and beautiful wife. When we played chess, his beautiful wife would serve us tea and cake, and he would say as she left the room that when he married her he thought he could teach her something, but that she had turned out to be plain dumb – she couldn't learn anything and he couldn't teach her anything. Had he made this confession to my father? Shocked that he would let his new, young wife witness him speak these insults, I was distressed. But I returned to the house many times.

I think I kept going back even when my brother's lessons had ceased. I was half in love with the man's wife, and I hated him. He was large and pushy, his heavy eyes glistening with self-satisfaction. He liked above all to be able to impress a small boy with his big talk. After a while, I thought I understood that in fact my father considered him a fool, and that I must be just as much a fool in my father's eyes if I sought this man's company.

Perhaps it was some overly rigid discipline adopted from his military years or an earlier implacable standard he identified with, for when leaving to go to school in the mornings, it had to be with hair brushed, ties tied, caps and hats straight, and shoes polished. 'You might be able to learn Latin but you can't even learn to polish your shoes,' he would say to me. And in a bloody-minded way, I became happy enough to construct a rough version of myself around that accusation. Perhaps the humiliation of it remains as a shadow, a provocation and a point of pride for me. He held us close, but he held us in contempt.

Does his silence about his father (and, in fact, his whole childhood), and that seeming eagerness to be gone into the army as a teenager, speak of damage done well before he became a soldier in a war? This would be another story, and much of it would have to be fiction.

The one value my father held to as a near-absolute was tribal loyalty. How could it be that we were Catholics (with the moral absolutes that came with that), but no matter how un-Christian or how 'sinful' one of us might be, my father's loyalty to family would come above all? And yet it was inside the family where he let his temper and venom loose. None of it made sense.

His obsession with sexual morality was equally intense. Politicians and public figures were judged on their fidelity in marriage. The increasing public disgrace of the Catholic Church for prolonged and incomprehensible abuse of children in their care confronted him. In the last year of his life, my father did try to tell me something about his experience of abuse, perhaps impulsively as a plea for understanding, or more likely to prove some point important and urgent for him at the time.

He talked of a family friend who used to visit their home and get drunk and stay the night. He said the man climbed into his childhood bed with him, so he understood what men could do to children. That was all. Perhaps he was showing me the world could teach him little he didn't already know. He went on to some other topic, some other complaint. He had made his point – about vulnerability, knowledge, men's evil, even perhaps about the failure of parents to protect their children in his story that was so brief it was not even a story.

While working on this essay I have been reading, among a half-dozen other books, Jess Hill's report on research into domestic abuse, *See What You Made Me Do*. I realise that my childhood home was sometimes a prison and sometimes a haven. Each day as I returned from school and each morning as I woke in that place, I couldn't be sure which it would turn out to be.

My father believed he understood men, a conviction that could bring you forcefully in under his orbit. As long as he could see you as a type, he had you, even if it took him a few wrong guesses to get you right. Then you were pocketed.

His best years were his time in business managing teams of hot-asphalt spreaders. The workers were mostly Italians who loved him and were devoted to him. In my last couple of years at school during the mid-1960s, I did labouring work with them through the summer and they told me what a good boss my father was. They bestowed on me some of the affection and loyalty they felt towards him. I was in another world with them, a place where my father was trusted, where something like love passed between him and these men, a place where migrant families saw him as their avenue to success and dignity. I was proud to be the son of such a man – and upset at him for not bringing these qualities into his own family. What happened to him in our presence? What was it that brought out such desperate meanness when he was with us? There was something about family life that could turn him inside out with rage.

Sometimes, though, he was that generous father I craved and imagined. He could take us into the countryside for hikes and picnics, or to the beach in summer where he liked to swim out until he was a far smudge on the sea. For a while, there were purple-eyed ferrets caged in the backyard. I remember going ferreting with him and his mates, setting the nets at rabbit-hole entrances across a paddock, then letting a ferret into a burrow and waiting for the rabbits to come racing in a panic up and out and into those nets, where they would be easy to grab and have their necks wrung.

Sometimes, though, a ferret would settle with its catch inside a burrow, refusing to emerge. It was then that each person had to guard an entrance while someone began digging down to where the ferret was guarding its kill. It was chaotic, messy, hit and miss. But it did put rabbits on our table, and for a while we ate rabbit as often as people eat chicken now. I think it was at this half-wild life of mucking about in the open air with other men, making up the rules as you went, that my father found himself most fully.

In January 1945, his extra parachutist pay was cancelled, with a note on his file indicating he was unfit for marching or for long standing due to a 'stiff foot'. Nevertheless, in October, Leo managed to join a group reassigned to embark for Singapore. They visited Changi Prison and contributed a contingent of troops to a guard of honour for the official surrender. Until January 1946, they operated as local military police preventing looting while order was restored to Singapore.

Then, on 29 May 1946, private Leo was discharged without ceremony back into civilian life. He had been in the military for most of the first eight years of his early adulthood, and upon resuming his civilian status, his home address was still his parents' address in Coburg. By September 1949, he would be married, with a two-year-old daughter and me, his new baby boy. Seven more children would follow.

How unprepared was this erratic, restless young soldier for the life that he found himself choosing so soon after the war? In her chapter on the experiences of children in families where fathers are abusive, Hill writes of a form of post-traumatic stress suffered by combat veterans:

> Every time a potential threat arises a survival response triggers in the brain, motivating the soldier to act defensively – a reaction that can be the difference between life and death.

This describes my father's reaction when faced with a crisis or even a passing difficulty within the family. He could react as if his physical life depended upon him fighting his way through to an immediate victory – darkly red in the face, veins striking lines down his neck, green eyes alive with an animal urge to survive no matter what damage might be done to others. It was easy to be terrified of him at these times.

Was this reaction fixed in him by the cumulative terrors of the bombing raids over Darwin, the repeatedly suppressed panic he must have faced in jumping from planes, the shock of seeing mates die in accidents, the physical and psychological rigours of training among men renowned for their wildness – and by feelings of grief and guilt over the death of his brother Bernie? He kept a photo of Bernie on his desk all his adult life. How far beyond his temperamental limits might he have been tested during those shaping years of his early twenties? I suspect there was as much shame as pride for him in his war experience, and more confusion than purpose.

Larrikin or patriarch? Trouble-maker or law-giver? Working man or thinker? Tribal lord or obedient Catholic parishioner? Scheming insider or cynical outsider? Husband or knockabout? Survivor or warrior? He loved telling stories, and he was good at it, but some form of confused shame, I think, kept him from telling the stories that were closest to him, which were the ones I wanted to hear.

The almost daily violence at home continued through my childhood in part because we kept it among ourselves. There I was, silent, arriving at school of a morning shamed by bruised legs, and there were the teachers keeping their distance. The vicious dog our neighbour kept in his tiny yard was no less loud, mad and wrong than my father. But nobody complained about either of them. There might have been no words for what was happening. Now I write what I can in the hope of coming somewhere close to comprehending how my father might have been as a young man bursting with himself while struggling, as I imagine him, between recklessness and fear, cowardice and bravado, all the while desperate to keep himself intact as much as a green young man could in that wartime world. I am writing this with an eye out for the ways my imagined father might point me away from a shamed, inchoate privacy that can only make each of us diminished versions of ourselves.

There is a surviving, faded, black-and-white photo of him with a mate who remained a lifelong friend. They are in Darwin on the wharves, both dressed in loose-fitting tropics uniforms, helmets at cocky angles, my father's arm over his friend's shoulder as their bodies lean in towards each other.

Helmets at cocky angles … Leo and a lifelong friend
Source: Provided by the author.

My father's expression is easy, open, confident, untroubled. They look like men who have arrived in a place that suits them. This isn't the man I remember. But it's a man I'd like to get to know and spend time with. This is the man my mother must have loved so completely just a few years later. In the moment of the photo, he appears supremely comfortable with himself and with the kind of friendship made possible in that war zone.

Editor's note: This essay was shortlisted for the 2023 Calibre Essay Prize for an outstanding essay.